I0616087

My Buddy

Bali

A Tourist in
Kisses and Tears

∴° ✦ °∴

A Novel
Inspired in part by true-to-life events

Leu Seyer

Edited and illustrated by Miguel A. Reyes-Mariano
Proofread by Laura Antram – lauraantram@gmail.com
First edition: Sept. 17th, 2024. Rev.011725

LIBRARY OF CONGRESS CATALOGING IN PUBLICATIONS DATA
Seyer, Leu

My Buddy Bali: A Tourist in Kisses and Tears.
In 2051, a seven-month-old Corgi named Bali, full of liveliness, ran away from his residence in Toronto, Canada, in a quest for freedom and ventures. He fell into the hands of two young pickpockets who planned to steal small valuables in Toronto and resell them in New York City. In his run-off, Bali constantly faces adversities created by inconsequential human activities, the so-called progress. He clashed with Climate change and the uncoordinated advances in new modes of flying transportation. During his journey, he stumbled into the house of genius scientists. Unbeknownst to him, their experimental capsule teleported him to the closest parallel dimension. During teleportation, an artificial intelligence microchip unintentionally left inside the device merged animal and machine intelligence into one living being. This helped manage his landing in the soap opera the scientist's son's girlfriend was watching on television. The episode was a rerun of the award-winning South Korean melodrama "Kisses and Tears" from 2042.

ISBN in Back-Cover

Printed in the United States of America

My Buddy Bali

A lighthearted account of the adventures of a Corgi puppy through an ever-scenario yet surreal dimensional travel... surprising, witty, and mystic! — Enilda Pires-PhD

Table Of Contents

Bali's Short-lived Escaped 3

Bali Runs Away from Home 20

Bali Back to The Road 39

Bali Found a Friend 61

Bali Goes Back to The Future 83

The Story of Motuo and David 102

Bali is Not Coming Back Home 119

Seven and a Half Months Earlier 134

Bali's Memorable Moments 151

Bali Escaped

To Another Dimension 175

The Epilogue 195

Trivia About Corgis' Tails III

Afterword by

Enilda Mougenot Pires-PhD* VII

Acknowledgment XII

Book One

---•☆•---

Balis' Grand Escape

Bali's Short-lived Escaped

At first glance, this story may appear like many others you have likely read before. The language, the tone, and the sentence structure may seem repetitive and predictable. Or perhaps the little black box of Noam Chomsky[1] could have generated original content (others may think). That is to say, this is a possibility, although writers keep repeating the same limited number of words (in the English language) all the time. Moreover, you might be assuming I am about to recount a tale similar to one you have already read. However, one crucial aspect sets this story apart from all the rest of the fantasy or science-fiction stories you have read or will ever read in the future.

The unique element of this story, akin to each living being's distinct pupils and fingers-or-nose prints, is that two of the main characters are based on a factual person and her puppy (these are not fictional). Billy, lovingly known as Bali, was Dr. Tatiana's constant furry companion. There was no moment in Tatiana's life when Bali was not at her side. Whether having a meal, taking a walk in the park, running errands, going to appointments, or even going to sleep, Bali was always there. Woefully, in reality and fantasy, Bali's fate mirrored each other. In his mischievous way, he slipped from Tatiana's loving home and arms to embark on a journey to a faraway dimension. But let us start from the very beginning of this fantastic story instead.

It all started on a peaceful winter morning when the sun slowly ascended above the horizon, casting a warm glow over the sleeping city. The sky was a vast expanse of clear blue without a single cloud in sight, and the breeze carried a subtle chill with it. On his morning walk, a Corgi puppy, about seven months old and full of boundless energy, pranced through the soft grass. His ears perked up at the cheerful chirping of birds nestled in their tree homes nearby.

As he strolled along, his tiny paws crinkled the dry leaves that lay scattered on the path, filling his sensitive nose with the scents of nature. While he could have frolicked and played to his heart's content, he walked calmly instead, taking in the sunrise's beauty as its rays kissed his golden facial fur and warmed his small body. His pace was unhurried, filled only with contentment and joy as he reveled in his morning stroll.

Out of the blue and without warning, a small rabbit leaped into the path of the puppy Corgi, causing the confused pup to jerk his head back and forth in surprise. The bunny came to a graceful stop as if waiting for the Corgi's reaction. In an instant, the pup barked frantically and took off after the bunny with determination, fueled by his incredible speed. The chase was on, with the puppy zigzagging and darting around minor obstacles in his pursuit of the elusive bunny. Too much stuff was on the side of the roads, like the speed limit signs, crash barriers, and all kinds of junk drivers throw out. Suddenly, with a swift turn to the right, the cunning Corgi outmaneuvered the bunny, causing him to spin around in confusion and move left into the road.

Undeterred, the energetic puppy continued his pursuit without missing a beat until he suddenly made a sharp left turn toward the bustling highway. The bunny's agility was on full display, leaving all who witnessed it in awe of his abilities. Although, the chaos created was 'I M P R E S S I V E.'

"ScreeeeeeeeeeK... BANG! WhiirrrrrrrrrK... BANG! KablammmmmnG!" A sudden sound of screech from a hard brake echoed in the little Corgi's ears. All the little birds sitting on the electric power lines flew away quickly. A 'rolling noise,' more like a drumming of tires on the dry asphalt roads, filled the space in the next 162 feet (49.38 meters) of pavement.

The sound of metals clashing and the smell of burning tires filled the air. In a couple of minutes, about 15 cars crashed going northwest and another 12 going southeast. Autonomous vehicles could stop before hitting the next, but the total number of entirely manual cars still running on the highways couldn't react on time. Besides, the car that flipped over the longitudinal barriers that separated the opposing traffic on this divided highway made a tremendous difference.

That electric car was a semi-autonomous flying car with the ability to deploy a safety parachute in the event of an accident. It turned out that the driver was controlling the vehicle manually. So, when he tried to avoid the rabbit, he took off into the air at the exact moment when another flying-mobile was already passing over him in that airspace. The collision was minor on the **left** end of the vehicle, except the other conveyance was coming too fast, and the impact projected his car onto the other side of the highway. To avoid being inside his pairs of wheels when it fell on the asphalt, the driver deployed a compressed air-powered parachute for escape maneuvers, and he landed safely off the road.

Nonetheless, his electric sedan was almost immediately hit by an autonomous truck carrying all kinds of toys for dogs. The quantity and variety of doggy toys were huge. A sample of a red, inflatable bouncing ball, made of an impenetrable material inside the main cabin, escaped after the windows broke on the impact with the concrete lane dividers. This ball rolled down the highway, bouncing into every object it encountered. It bounced down the roads, passing over uneven grounds and street intersections, until the last spin reached the front of the corner side deck in the **house of the little Corgi puppy's owners, less than seven miles (about 11 kilometers) from the accident.**

The car accident was both shocking and stunning, with twisted metal and skid marks covering the pavement. Some other drivers passing by through the air space had even deployed their parachutes to escape because of the chaos and confusion. Now, broken plastic debris lay scattered on the sides of the highway. Thankfully, advanced technology has dramatically improved over time, protecting the drivers more than the vehicles involved. Only a few commuters suffered minor cuts or concussions as their out-of-date airbags deployed or from impact with the foam padding inside the cars from the mere collision with other vehicles. Fortunately, no one was critically injured, a testament to the effectiveness of modern safety measures.

The highway patrolmen, decked in their gleaming electric manual-flying cars, arrived at the scene with remarkable speed. The flashing orange, red, and blue lights of the patrol cars illuminated the sky and were visible even on that sunny sunrise, conveying the gravity of the accident to all who passed by. They acted as a barrier, preventing other aerial vehicles from entering the area. Also, the ambulances in their sun-powered 'Airship Balloons' expedited their way to the accident. News channels buzzed around in their small electric drone cars, capturing every angle of the chaotic scene. Their miniature drones darted through the air, capturing the most minor details of the accident.

The firefighters came on their 'Hum Riders,' raised almost 14 feet (4.27 meters) into the air, moving through the rest of the traffic without delay. They had a bird's-eye view of the wreckage and could swiftly rescue any injured person trapped inside. Amidst all the chaos and commotion, the friendly little canine made his way back through the small state park that led him to the road. After trekking less than three miles (4.83 kilometers), he stumbled upon his own town. This fortunate canine miraculously found an opening underneath the fence meant to keep pedestrians out of the highway — most likely dug by another clever animal.

Bali wasn't completely the one to blame. Recognizing the social transformation since mid-2040 is crucial. There's a saying that claims chaos is a necessary precursor to substantial changes. It is widely believed that individuals only adjust to changes once the new additions become customary in the system. By 2050, the global economy had fully embraced renewable energy and witnessed the widespread adoption of flying electric cars. Yet, car accidents became very common without the corresponding costly infrastructure adjustments.

Despite this accident, life moved forward, and Bali, sooner than later, left to return home. As Bali returned to the city, calm seemed to have returned to planet Earth. He could hear the sirens in the distance and was already far away from the bustle and chaos of the traffic accident. Once again, he rejoined the placid walk he had started before sunrise. **About 97 minutes had passed since he left his house for a** walk that Saturday morning. Of course, he had to run a little, chasing a frog before he found that small state park and then a little more to get out of it quickly. Despite that, he had already regained his breath, and his peaceful steps were leading him back home — only if he would not get distracted on his way back.

While he was enjoying his walk, other people were working at a small facility near the state park. It was more like an industrial plant where not too many people worked at, based on the number of cars parked in the parking lot—or it could be what the passersby might have thought. The sign outside reads, "Locus Enterprise, LLC." The little Corgi dog did not know where he was going but did not get distracted by the warning signs either. There were many red and white, white and black, and yellow and black placards since he entered the parking lot. Even so, letters or colors didn't make any difference to him. His adventurous spirit wanted to discover the mystery in front of him. "What was inside that building?" That was inside his head, and he would not quit until he found out.

The property housed a small-scale industrial facility, resembling a micro or, better said, "nano nuclear plant," with little to minimal nuclear equipment fixed in the back area. The main building had three floors, and the basement had a separate entrance. Another structure was hidden in the back beneath a double reinforced concrete structure at the end of the property, near a small lake in the state park. The curious little Corgi couldn't resist exploring the building despite more warning signs posted in black and yellow and even black and red.

During the plant's inauguration, the company's marketing director advertised this unique space as a crucial part of a complex process. Their undertaking involved transferring/teleporting objects in their state of matters reduced to their sub-nanoparticles to different locations within a defined coordinate and time. Some pamphlets left at the reception still contained this information. The ultimate goal was to "transfer goods from a warehouse directly to buyers' homes, incurring no extra transportation costs." That was the business vision.

"Kwayyyyyyyyyyk... BOOM! Urrrrrrrrrrrth... CRACK! TthuuuuuuuuuuuuD... CLANG!" All of a sudden, once the little Corgi finally got into the building and was on his way to the center of the lab, the building collapsed. A sudden blast echoed throughout the facility, causing glass and metal to shatter and rubble to roll across the floor. The ground shook with high-frequency vibrations, making everyone who worked that day panic. The facility's alarm immediately sent out an emergency call for help, summoning rescue teams already dealing with the string of car accidents nearby. Thankfully, only the decorative structures sustained irreparable damage because of its unique construction design. In contrast, the central and basement installations' vital support structures for managing the nano nuclear plant remained intact.

Even though all the second and third floors of the building collapsed on top of the first floor, practically destroying it, it wasn't completely obliterated. The destruction that demolished the office space and the computing center also trapped 15 scientists working on a top-secret project that morning. They all were in the first-floor conference room when the explosion occurred. Among them, there was also a Corgi puppy who also got trapped in the middle of that chaos.

It was terrifying after the enormous 'boom' and the building falling. The pup barked a lot until there was no more breath on him. For the initial seven minutes, the noise inside the building was enough to deafen everyone. Howbeit, as quickly as it began, the loud noise abruptly ceased, leaving an eerie silence in its wake. The tyke dog cautiously poked his head out from behind a fallen wooden pillar, his heart pounding hard in his chest. The room became filled with smoke and debris, and the air grew heavy with a mixed burnt smell from the metal and electrical cables.

Everything happened so fast! Some people got hurt, but the majority got lucky because they sat next to one of the strongest columns that held up the ceiling where they were chatting in the conference room. The little pup's heart kept racing as dust and debris filled the air, making it hard to see or breathe. He quickly scanned the chaotic scene, his instincts kicking in. An uninjured scientist spots the Cardigan Welsh Corgi. They partnered, and both started rescuing others. Without a second thought, both rushed toward the injured, helping them to safety amid the chaos. As they guided a young woman with a bruised arm toward an open space, she noticed a figure lying trapped under a fallen wood beam.

"Help me!" the man cried out, his voice strained with pain and anguish. The scientist didn't hesitate. With a grunt, he heaved against the heavy beam, muscles straining as he pushed with all his might. Others came to help, and inch by inch, the beam shifted until, finally, the man was free. "Thank you," the man gasped, tears of relief in his eyes. The puppy gave him a nod.

Finally, the fifteen of them were out of risk and ready to leave the building. But… "Where is the exit?" one of them asked. A resounding silence filled the space.

"I have an idea," said the canine's friend. "Let's follow the dog's lead."

Everyone agreed, and as soon as they all started moving, the man said to the little Corgi, "Let's go for a walk. 'Let's go!'"

The little puppy seemed to understand the message and wasted no time in sniffing around for the entrance of fresh air into the enclosure. This fresh air was a stark contrast to the heavy, stagnant air inside the room. It carried hints of nature, perhaps from the small state park and adjacent artificial lake nearby. Step by step, the little hound approached the origin of the fresh air. He could have easily escaped independently; even so, his instinct led him to find the best route for his human companions to fit through. As he advanced, the meadow-like scent of wildflowers and dew surrounded him, calming his nerves and giving him the strength to continue his quest.

As they moved closer to the fresh air source, the Corgi's heart pounded faster in his chest. He desperately dashed toward a viable exit to hit a dead end because his new friends could not escape through such a small hole. However, the deafening wails of sirens from fire trucks, police cars, and ambulances only grew louder, filling their ears with an eerie cacophony. The blaring noise ricocheted off the remnants of the demolished building, sending shivers down their spines.

Amid the chaos and destruction, flashing red and blue lights relentlessly illuminated the smoke-filled air, casting an ominous glow over the rubble. The chaotic rush of emergency responders only added to the overwhelming sense of danger and devastation surrounding them like a suffocating blanket.

Our little Corgi, with his big ears and sensitive nose, remained calm as he searched for a way out of the disaster. He navigated around corners, and his followers moved some debris in their relentless quest to find an escape route for themselves. Finally, he reached a section at the northwest corner of the building, where only a few pieces of wood blocked their path. Without hesitation, the pup bolted toward the shadows of what seemed like rescuers, and by sheer chance, the firefighters spotted him and rushed to his side. He barked incessantly and clawed his paws on their pants as if pleading for them to follow him—to help him. So, the firefighters followed his lead and found all 15 employees who were working at the plant on that Saturday morning.

The news channels had shifted their focus from the multiple-car crash to the vicinity of the plant explosion. They arrived at the time when the heroic Cardigan Welsh Corgi emerged from the building, seeming to beg for help from the firefighters in rescuing the 15 people trapped under the rubble of the collapsed building. The explosion that caused this destruction was a mystery, and its origin was unknown, but at least there was no evidence of nuclear spills, significant injuries, or missing people.

As smoke billowed out from the wreckage, an eerie silence filled the air, broken only by shouts and sirens of the first responders in the area. The scene was chaotic and frantic, with bystanders rushing to offer aid while emergency responders worked tirelessly to see if there were more people trapped as they didn't know for sure who was there in the first place. This event imprinted a memory on this little pup, the trapped scientists, and maybe the bystanders who witnessed it.

Nearly two hours had passed since this beloved puppy went out for a morning walk. Now, multiple cameras captured his every move and broadcast it to the world. This fantastic puppy bounded through the debris and wreckage with unbridled energy on every step. The commentators praised his bravery and analyzed how he saved the lives of those trapped inside the building's ruins. Miraculously, they escaped thanks to our furry hero's quick thinking and selflessness.

A few minutes after everyone had evacuated the plant's ruins, a second explosion shook the area, completely destroying what remained of the already devastated building. The once sturdy structure now lay in a pile of rubble while the brave pup remained unscathed. It was a moment that would forever live in the news records as an example of our canine friends' true heroism and loyalty.

The adorable Cardigan Welsh Corgi puppy was the star of the Saturday morning news at 9:00 AM; his slight frame illuminated screens nationwide on different news networks. "Breaking news," announced the anchor on Channel Seven, his voice filled with urgency. "A heroic puppy has saved the lives of 15 scientists at the Locus Enterprise nano nuclear plant here in Toronto, Canada."

Live shots from the scene showed the remains of the plant, still smoking and chaotic. As viewers woke up and tuned in to their TVs, they saw the brave canine who had performed this miraculous feat. The viewers were greeted with a heartwarming sight—a fluffy doggy wagging his tail and eagerly greeting the rescue workers.

"Oh, my goodness!" exclaimed one viewer from her living room, recognizing the friendly pet as her own beloved pooch called 'Bali.' "How did he end up there?" she wondered in disbelief and admiration for the little hero. "Babe, come to see this! It's Bali here on the 9:00 a.m. news on Channel Seven," the doggy owner commented to her husband.

"How did he manage to get out?" the husband responded in perplexity and amazement.

The husband's voice was grave as he turned to his wife. "We need to go to pick up Bali. He is our doggy, and we need to bring him home." The husband's voice took on a serious tone as he spoke, his words laced with urgency. "First things first. We need to get ready. Are you ready? Well, if you are ready, let's go."

His wife's face mirrored his concern as she stood up and reached for her wide-brimmed outdoor anti-UV hat.

"When we get back home, I'm calling the construction company to check the fence and fix any holes or imperfections. This can't happen again." His determination was palpable in every word, his hand tightening around the brim of his hat. They wore hats and sunglasses, although it was winter in Toronto, Canada.

As they set off toward their destination, the husband led the way with swift, purposeful strides while his wife followed closely behind, her resolute expression but calm.

Dr. Manuel Hashbun, an anesthesiology doctor at Toronto General Hospital, and his wife, Dr. Tatiana, a lawyer and university professor specializing in commercial law, went to their City Police Station to claim ownership of their Corgi named Bali—the doggy seen on Channel Seven's morning news at 9:00 a.m.

When they arrived at the precinct, it was around 9:45 AM. The receptionist asked them to wait while she tried to locate the dog. After waiting for 39 minutes at the front desk, the receptionist informed them that a detective would be with them shortly. Twenty-seven minutes later, Mr. and Mrs. Hashbun were feeling frustrated and anxious. Finally, Detective Campbell approached the couple and assured them he would 'personally' contact Dr. Manuel once he had the dog at the police station.

Soon after the Hashbuns arrived home, Dr. Manuel immediately instructed his computer assistant to contact both his security services agent and the construction company that sold them their house. By coincidence, they both arrived after lunch to address Dr. Manuel's concerns. They quickly searched through the security camera footage, revealing that there was no need for fence repairs; Bali had jumped onto a nearby trash can and then over the fence to land on the grass in front of the house.

"Thank you, gentlemen, for solving the mystery," Dr. Manuel said gratefully to the two men he had summoned. "However, I would still like to have some metal mesh added around the edges of the fence in the back of the house, as I noticed some small holes, and this will prevent Bali from escaping through there," he added with a nod. Later, both gentlemen bid their farewells before leaving the Hashbun's residence.

"Tring tring… Tring tring… Tring tring." The wireless home phone ringing echoed throughout the house's first floor before Tatiana finally answered it. It was Detective Campbell from the police station, notifying them that Bali was waiting for them at the precinct. It was around 3:53 PM. The detective added that they would need to sign some paperwork and register the puppy, as the one they had previously registered did not match Bali's description. He told them to be sure to bring some pieces of evidence of ownership. The detective also mentioned that the mayor wanted to recognize Bali publicly for his heroic actions and that he would contact them again with the date for the ceremony.

Without hesitation, the Hashbuns gathered all the necessary documents and made their way to the police station to pick up their furry companion. By the time they gathered all

17

the required documents, drove to the police station, and completed all the paperwork before returning home, it was already 6:02 PM. They celebrated Bali's bravery with exceptional food for him and playtime in the backyard, where he loved spending time with them. Bali loved his present, the indestructible red inflatable bouncing ball, and played tirelessly with it until he was exhausted. He would hit it with his nose, and Dr. Manuel would kick it back to him in whatever way possible.

"When did we buy this red ball for Bali?" Dr. Manuel asked.

"I don't remember ever having seen it before," Tatiana replied.

Without further ado, they continued playing with him for some time, commemorating his heroic day.

As the sun began its slow descent toward the horizon at dusk, its warm rays beat down upon the face of Bali, the Hashbun's tricolor Cardigan Welsh Corgi puppy. He certainly has a peaceful life in the Hashbun's residence. Bali's owners lived in a prosperous suburban neighborhood outside Toronto, Canada's bustling metropolis. Even though it was winter in Canada, climate change brought them warm temperatures. This was the eighth winter in a row without snow in the northern region of America, with only occasional flurries that quickly melted away in a few hours. The last significant snowfall in that part of the world was in November 2042, almost a decade ago. The only resemblance to a traditional winter in these times was the sight of leaves gently falling and being carried by the wind through the streets of Toronto.

- - -

[1]Chomsky, N. (2014). *Aspects of the theory of syntax, 50th anniversary edition*. MIT Press.

Bali Runs Away from Home

A month later, well into that warm winter season, with skies as lucid as a clear crystal and the sun shining down like a beacon of warmth, Bali strolled along the white wooden fence that bordered his house, one of the grand homes in this upscale neighborhood. At seven and half months old, his golden face fur glimmered in the sunlight and contrasted perfectly with his white chest and short, double-waterproof fur. His back and part of his loin were of a deep-dark black, reminiscent of the color "vantablack," first developed in 2014, which seemed to mimic a black hole's appearance as this pigment absorbed 99.97% of the light.

But what truly made Bali stand out were his piercing blue left eye and medium-sized, undocked tail, both rare features for his breed, adding to his unique charm. The breeder mentioned that he also has a little pink birthmark on the left bottom lip–nothing to worry about. As he roamed freely through his home's backyard, Bali's paws practically tingled with excitement at the sight of a girl riding her bright pink bicycle around the nearby streets. He couldn't avoid barking effusively, filled with an intense desire to chase after her and explore every corner of the world with her by his side.

Not too far away, the girl could hear a doggy's loud, sharp barking in the distance. She halted abruptly, her bike wheels squeaking to a halt on the pavement. Turning back toward the source of the noise, she saw a small Corgi in the backyard of one house not very distant from her. A rush of excitement and curiosity overtook her as she came closer to get a better look. The little canine had one blue eye and one brown eye, creating a unique and endearing gaze that seemed to lock onto hers with intense focus, sparking a connection she couldn't ignore.

Suddenly, Bali let out a fierce growl and barked playfully, inviting her to join him in a game of chase. However, it was time for the girl to head home, though she now knew of this friendly furry neighbor. Bali couldn't understand why she had to leave and continued to bark and howl, his determination shining through. He made sure she heard him until she disappeared down the narrow street in front of his home.

"Calm down, Bali!" his owner's voice echoed from inside the house, a mixture of frustration and exasperation.

"That dog never seems to learn!" her husband joined in, frustration lacing his words. "What was all that money we spent on training for?"

Meanwhile, Bali groaned in dissatisfaction and scratched his claws against the wooden fence posts, his longing for freedom palpable. As he gazed out beyond the confines of his backyard, he could see an entirely new world waiting to be explored—the winding streets of the neighborhood, filled with bikes and children playing under the shining sun. His heart raced with excitement as he yearned to join in on the fun and adventure beyond his sheltered existence.

As he perceived a noise, he started moving with fierce determination; Bali raced up the oak tree on the front west side of the house, barking ferociously at the squirrel darting out of reach. His breath came in sharp, excited pants as adrenaline coursed through his veins. The squirrel responded with angry whimpers, taunting him from a safe distance. Bali's playfulness knew no bounds. He continued to bark and growl effusively, his eyes narrowed in a menacing glare. Desperate to catch his challenger, he leaped toward the tree trunk, only to slip and crash back down to the ground on all fours. Still on high alert, Bali's tail remained rigid and motionless as he tracked the squirrel's every move, his playful spirit undiminished.

Perched atop the high gnarled branches of the ancient angel oak, the squirrel watched with beady eyes as Bali's uproar filled the air. His barks mingled with the rustling of leaves and the frantic chirping of birds, creating a dissonance that pierced through the quiet neighborhood. Still, the squirrel remained unfazed and defiant even as it chattered back in shrill squeaks while his tail twitched in agitation.

The squirrel's sharp chittering echoed through the branches as Bali's barking reached a fever pitch. His tail wagged furiously, kicking up grass clippings and leaves around him in his excitement. Bali's eyes sparkled with mischief as he leaped at the base of the massive oak tree, trying to glimpse the chatty squirrel. His energy was infectious, and as he continued his barking frenzy, some passersby stopped to witness such fierce disruption in that neighborhood.

The next-door neighbor, who didn't like the Hashbuns very much, yelled for Bali to shut up so loudly and thunderously that others thought burglars had broken into her home. The distance between the houses was quite significant, but she always spied on what was happening in that house. However, for some mysterious reason, Bali's owners did not hear a single bark until everything was already pandemonium.

Faced with the deafening cries of the old lady, another neighbor ran out with his rifle to see what was going on. Another passerby who saw this person armed immediately called the police. Within seven minutes, a patrol car was in the neighborhood, its lights flashing and sirens blaring. There was total confusion among those gathered there, and in the background, Bali continued to bark at full lungs. One by one, all the neighbors on the block came out of their houses and walked to Bali's house. Over 47 people gathered there because of Bali's disruptive dispute with the squirrel.

"Bannnnnnng!" The back door of the Corgi's home burst open, causing Bali to come back to his senses. He was so distracted by his quarreling with the squirrel that he hardly cared about the commotion of the people gathering there. The owner's voice echoed through the kitchen's walls in an authoritative tone, demanding Bali to stop whatever he was doing. Ears tucked back and tail between his legs, Bali scurried across the yard to his navy-blue bed, made of rough polyester, cold vinyl, and faux fur that, internally for him, it felt like sandpaper against his skin.

The police knocked on Hashbun's door. After an intense conversation with Tatiana and Manuel, the patrolman gave them a ticket for the public disturbance caused by the puppy. Meanwhile, those gathered outside talked among themselves, trying to understand what had happened. After the police officers left the house, they dispersed the crowd and ordered them to return home. Slowly, one by one, they left, and so they went until they all dispersed, and calm reigned again in the neighborhood.

After everybody had dispersed, Bali returned to his bed, which was not his preference nor the backyard that he considered his small confinement. Yet, Bali's bed was of the highest quality on the market, and the house was not small **at all—with over 4,700 square feet (436.61 square meters) of construction and almost two acres of land (0.81 hectare). It was a splendid house in an upper-class neighborhood. It had a complete maid's room, breakfast room next to the kitchen, two Livingroom in different levels, a library-studio, formal dining room, four bedrooms with bathrooms,**

24

one suite, and an additional informal dining room. There was also a multiple garage space on the half first floor for their fancy cars, including the flying electric semiautonomous vehicle.

It was clear that Bali's owners had plenty of wealth and space. Yet here he was—as he thought about his condition, confined to this limited existence, while others, like the squirrels and little rabbits, roamed free without a care in the world. This was enough to make Bali feel a deep despair inside him. It seemed that at seven months, every puppy yearned to explore and discover the world. But, if there were a partner to play with, things wouldn't be so bad—maybe. Besides, *"What happened to the girl I used to play with so much in the afternoons?"* was the concern on his mind sometimes.

"Where is that little girl?" he questioned himself, thinking perhaps that one afternoon she would return to play with him. Not the girl with the red bike, the eight-year-old girl who used to live in that house. Bali didn't know that her father had changed her afternoon arrangements since his father invited her to go fishing without notifying him. He was so angry that he finally had a nanny stay at his new house to care for his daughter, Elena, for almost 17 hours a day. He also installed an entire security camera system to monitor her constantly, and he trained her to press the panic **button in case of emergency and how to notify the police immediately if any unforeseen event occurred.**

But Bali never understood why she stopped coming to see him, and that definitely didn't help him contain his loneliness in the afternoons. Besides that, and despite the ample space in the house and patio, Bali still found it small compared to his aspirational dreams, as he had already explored everything there. Further, after the installation of the metallic net after his first short-lived escape, now not even small animals could get into the yard so that he could sniff their aromas from time to time. So, now he grunted and twisted in circles, trying to find a comfortable position in his bed most of his days.

The monotony of his daily routine weighed heavily on him. His owners were rarely home, leaving him to entertain himself with mundane activities since he was no longer allowed to play with the cat Zizzo after the incident with Dr. Hashbun's sofa. He missed the pretty girl who used to play with him the most, and he didn't understand why she had moved away. As he looked out the fence, he longed for the days when he could roam outside and chase after birds, bikes, cars, squirrels, or wild bunnies. His memories of those playful walks in the park with that little girl were filling him with a deep sense of nostalgia. The loneliness hit him hard, and he yearned dearly for companionship.

Routinely, day after day, Bali typically lay curled up in his bed, hidden under the substructure of the patio terrace in the backyard. One morning, his deep sighs echoed off the fence looming in front of the house, a barrier between him and the world beyond. In his mind, he imagined escaping from this place one day—running free and exploring unfamiliar sights and smells. The thought brought a glimmer of excitement to his eyes as he rested his head on his paws. As the sun began to rise and the house grew noisy, Bali carefully peered out from underneath the framework of the patio terrace. He could hear the faint chirping of birds roosting in the angel oak tree nearby. He went to the yard very early that day; his owner took him out earlier than usual.

A couple of hours later, thanks to the weather, his owners had come out to enjoy their morning coffee under the wooden gazebo. Dr. Manuel had a day off, and Dr. Tatiana called for a vacation day at her office. This gazebo stood proudly in the backyard, surrounded by lush green grass and colorful flowers. Despite the weathering and wear, the wooden frame of the gazebo stood firm and robust, showcasing its sturdiness and elegance. His owner, Tatiana, had added some shelves to place family pictures, and one of Bali was in one of those stands. A bigger one is in the living room of the house. Bali felt a warm sense of inclusion; sharing a family moment and briefly staring at his picture made him feel part of this lovely family, even if it was a temporary emotion.

That morning, thanks to his good behavior, Bali was allowed into the kitchen after breakfast. Once there, he noticed from the back of the kitchen that the front door was ajar. He paused and observed again to confirm that what he had seen was true.

"*This is it*," Bali thought.

Without wasting time, he ran as fast as he could to the door, his much-dreamed-of escape within reach. But, as he was about to take the last leap toward the house's entrance, some familiar hands caught him. "Where are you going, 'MY BUDDY BALI'?" The voice and the familiar essence belonged to the son of the house owners, Dr. Rafik Hashbun, who stopped there to pick up a correspondence that had arrived at that address for him.

"Woof, woof, woof." Bali's heart swelled with joy upon recognizing him, and he began to wag his tail frantically. His old friend, a source of comfort and joy, was here. He hoped to see his daughter, the eight-year-old girl he used to play with in the backyard in the afternoons. However, she did not visit him that day—what bad luck. His disappointment was palpable. Anyway, he forgot about his escape plans temporarily—at least for today— since he wanted to play with his old friend a little. Bali used to play a lot with his daughter in this house, which he moved into immediately after his divorce. However, he bought his own home because of differences of opinion about raising his offspring. This led to a distinct problem of finding a daycare for his eight-year-old daughter, as that was the price for maintaining his integrity.

"Son, Isabel called. She wants you to call her as soon as possible. She says it's urgent," Tatiana told her stepson Rafik, whom she always called 'Son.'

"But did she tell you what she wants, Mom?" Rafik asked his stepmother, whom he always called 'Mom.'

"No, just to tell you to call her as soon as possible," Tatiana answered.

"Okay, I'll call her later," Rafik concluded. Isabel was Dr. Rafik's first wife, and he didn't talk much about her. In fact, his daughter Elena recently found out that she was four years older than her dad.

Over the last six years, Toronto's temperature has increased by four degrees compared to the previous decade. On that warm winter day of January 19, 2051, Thursday's temperatures reached an unseasonably high of 71 degrees Fahrenheit (21.67 degrees Celsius). After the morning gathering, Bali lounged on his bed under the low terrace, basking in the warmth and daydreaming about his next **family days as if it was already summer there in Toronto.**

Following the sofa incident, he could only enter the house after six o'clock in the afternoon during these winter months until further notice. To pass the time, he trotted around the yard and sometimes played with butterflies near the trees at the end of the backyard. Those didn't have to migrate south that year or probably in previous years, either.

Later that day, Bali made his way to the front fence, **where he sniffed around for a potential escape point—that** was constantly throbbing in his mind. Oooh! What a thrill! He found a weak spot near the front angel oak tree, where the wood edges bottoms were getting rotten, and the fence posts where the roots grew surpassing it were crumbling a little in the fence's corner in the dividing line with the next property. This was not noticeable because of the surrounding bushes.

When he was about to start another escape attempt, his owner called out for dinner. "Come on, Bali! It's dinnertime," yelled his owner. The escape might have to wait another day —dinner goes first.

In front of the house, an aged maple tree stood almost in the middle of the house on Bali's owners' property, its branches reaching out as if to embrace the house's large front windows. A vibrant blue bird was perched at the tip of one branch, inches from the clear glass panes. Tirelessly, he collected twigs and leaves, carefully weaving them together to create a sturdy nest. Every day, he toiled away, adding more pieces to his creation. His beak moved with precision and grace as he navigated between branches or darted down to pick up fallen twigs off the ground.

As the nest took shape and grew more significant, the bird's anticipation of spring was palpable. He protected it fearlessly, knowing it would become a sanctuary for him, his devoted mate, and their future offspring. Despite the moderate winter chill, the sun shone brightly, warming his feathers as he worked. With each addition to his masterpiece, the little bird sang joyfully, his anticipation of spring evident on every note. As he was about to put the finishing touches on his home, he heard a soft chirp in the distance. He raised his head and spotted his partner approaching with eager excitement in her eyes. The little blue bird immediately reacted, making a loud, piercing sound of joy.

The wind was blowing strong that late afternoon, and it would seem as if the wind grabbed the maple branch to make it touch the glass of the house's front window at the time of the blue bird's piercing sound of joy. Tatiana and Bali were in the living room watching TV, and both turned their heads at the time of this sound. They end up drawn to watch as the birds meticulously finish building their nest, feeling a sense of connection to the couple's dedication to working toward their togetherness.

As Tatiana observed the birds' efforts, she couldn't help thinking of her own experiences in creating a home. She gave Bali a warm hug, mirroring the bond between the birds. Thus, instead of continuing to watch the soap opera, they both sat mesmerized by the construction of the nest, united with these tiny creatures in their common goal. The birds remained oblivious to their audience, focused only on completing their task to one day welcome a new life under Canada's endless blue skies.

The next day, the Friday morning of January 20, 2051, **was a beautiful one. The sun was rising and beginning to** shine in the clear blue sky, and a gentle breeze rustled through the leaves of the towering angel oak tree that stood proudly in Bali's front yard. After taking care of his business outside, Bali eagerly returned to the kitchen for breakfast.

He savored every bite of the special salmon ration mixed with small pieces of turkey and roasted chicken that his owner always prepared for him in the mornings. As he ended eating, his mind wandered to his favorite activity—escaping from his confining yard. With determination burning inside him, he bolted out of the house and made a beeline toward the corner of the fence, where he had slowly started digging a hole. Bali thought that these pieces of sticks were a temporary hindrance because nothing could calm his desire for freedom.

His paws scraped at the dirt and gnarled roots as he worked tirelessly to make his escape route. Each scratch and bite brought him closer to freedom. Then, when he thought he couldn't dig anymore, the fence wobbled and gave way, crumbling under his determined efforts. A couple of its sticks and the portions of the rotten root of the angel oak tree also crumbled a little more. Bali slipped through the small opening without hesitation and tumbled into the neighbor's yard. *"I am finally free!"* he expressed with a smile. Nonetheless, his excitement was very brief as a loud noise startled him. He looked up to see the neighbor glaring at him from her backyard. She wasted no time in trying to get him out of her space. Despite the incident, she didn't alert her neighbors because of their long-standing feud.

"Come on, get out of here!" that neighbor, the old lady, shouted. The piercing shrieks of the neighbor echoed through the air as she slammed her hands against the side gate of her house, desperately trying to force him out of her front yard. Her arms flailed wildly in a futile attempt to scare him off. The space between their two houses seemed like an endless stretch of green grass and white picket fences, a little more than a quarter of a football field apart (23 meters). Because they were absorbed in their leisurely breakfast, the homeowners inside Bali's house paid little to on-attention to their neighbor's commotion.

With a mischievous glint in his eyes, Bali darted back and forth in the neighbor's front yard, his tail wagging excitedly. The old lady's efforts to shoo him away only seemed to invigorate him further, as if her desperate attempts signaled a game of chase. When she threw one of her flip-flops at him and hit him on the back, he ran toward the safety of the front bushes in his neighbor's yard. Panic set in as he realized he couldn't go home because that would expose him. Besides, it would take time for him to dig back into the hole. Bali wasn't analyzing all this information, but **his instincts made it seem like he was studying it all.**

The neighbor walked back into her house to search for a broom to shoo him away. However, when she emerged again, she couldn't find him because he had hidden behind the bushes near the fence. He calculated his next move without flicking an ear to avoid getting chased. Bali's remarkable maturity, for being only seven and a half months old, was a testament to his intelligence and ability to comprehend human behavior. This earned him admiration as a member of his breed and as a smart animal—per se.

Frantically, he searched for another escape route, determined not to be caught and punished for his mischief. His eyes darted until they landed on the slightly open side door used to dispose of the domestic waste. He also spotted some big plastic containers, other small plastic boxes, and a few cardboard boxes in front of the house. **Without hesitation, he** dashed toward them, seeking refuge among the discarded rubbishes.

Bali, a small and agile dog, had been raised alongside a cat since he was a tiny puppy. Bali had to learn to jump high and enter through small holes so as not to let the cat escape with his toys or to let him hide all day when he wanted a partner to play with. So, he picked up some of the feline's behaviors over time, including the ability to jump over more than three feet (almost one meter) high. However, some things continue to puzzle him, such as why his owners didn't allow the cat to play with him in the backyard or why he needed to use the sandbox. He had seen nobody else using it. Anyhow, Bali didn't have time for those thoughts as he focused on his latest escape plan.

With determination in his eyes, Bali bounded toward the garbage containers at the side end of the garbage bins on the sidewalk by the old lady's house. He leaped into a nearby plastic bin using a discarded old armchair as a launching pad. He landed over a discarded medium-sized plastic box filled with old newspapers and magazines near the other end of the pile, along with the cardboard boxes. It **was his lucky day— his escape coincided with the trash collection day for their residential sector. The rumbling** sound of approaching garbage trucks echoed through the streets already.

While mechanical hands were collecting standard trash cans, manual labor was still required for the collection of certain recycling materials. This task was purposely left for humans to ensure employment opportunities, even if it meant extra effort and longer journeys for those who worked for the government. Bali knew none of this as he happily hopped between piles of boxes and containers, feeling like he was in control of his adventure's next move.

Bali rarely paid much attention to the garbage trucks and collectors, only barking at them on collection day.

Anyhow, on this day, he watched with a fierce determination to ensure a safe escape, driven by a stronger will than any potential obstacles in his way. The garbage truck rumbled down the quiet Toronto Street, its metal claws clinking as they reached out to grab another bin. Bali's eyes looked to the top of the bin in expectation, his heart pounding in excitement.

In any other unfamiliar situation, Bali would have darted into the busy street without a moment's hesitation. Now, with the threat of an attack from his neighbor or the intimidating garbage collectors looming over him, fear coursed through his tiny body as he searched frantically for a safe place to plan his following actions.

As he crouched in the recycling box, trying to make himself as small and unnoticeable as possible, the sound of approaching footsteps made his heart race faster. Without warning, the garbage collector lifted the plastic box, and Bali's eyes met those of the surprised Canadian public employee working for the municipality of that sector.

But Bali sprung out of the plastic box before the man could react. It was an unusual gesture for a man of his **occupation, a garbage collector, to show any sign of affection to a completely unknown dog. However**, it was evident that occupation has nothing to do with a person's character. Bali only glanced at him and got impressed and a little scared. He was a tall, mocking figure with broad shoulders and a permanent scowl etched onto his face. His dirty, bright yellow overalls hung loosely on his muscular frame, and his hands were large and calloused from years of manual labor. A thick dark mustache sat above his mouth, a thin-lipped one, adding to his intimidating appearance. Yet, in a minuscule moment of inaction, he felt an unexpected affection toward Bali. "Maybe it's his contagious joy," he thought.

"Stop playing with that puppy and finish picking up that trash!" his colleague shouted after him, annoyed at his apparent playfulness while they were trying to do their job. Taking advantage of the distraction, Bali dashed across the street and disappeared into the bushes on the other side of the inner street—thank God for vegetation.

The thrill of his daring escape ran through Bali's veins as he found himself roaming freely on the streets. He managed to escape from both his own backyard and his nosy neighbor's. Now, with endless possibilities ahead of him, Bali excitedly pondered, "Where to go next? As long as I stay one step ahead." With a sly smile, he thought, "I can conquer anything."

Later on, Bali cautiously poked his head out of the lush green bushes lining the internal street of the residential neighborhood. The morning was peaceful and serene, with only the faint sound of distant traffic lingering in the air after the daily garbage trucks had passed through. Bali's mismatched brown and bright left-blue eyes scanned his surroundings before he boldly decided, "It's time to take the next step!"

With a burst of energy, he sprang out of the bush and darted across the sidewalk, heading south of his home on the opposite side of the street. His tail swished back and forth with uncontainable happiness at the sight of his familiar surroundings.

The sun was already shining brightly on the neighborhood, casting warm rays of light onto the neatly manicured lawns and colorful houses. It was almost 7:39 a.m. this sunny Friday morning, and most residents were beginning their day. Some residents were finishing breakfast in their cozy kitchens while others hurriedly dropped off their children at the school bus stop before heading to work. A few lucky individuals were leisurely strolling along the street, perhaps on their way to grab a cup of coffee before returning to work in the comfort of their own homes. As for Bali, he scampered along with excitement as he finally was in control of his destinations.

Bali's mind shifted from deciding whom to follow to pondering what to do next. His nose quivered with anticipation as he took in all the unfamiliar scents around him. From blooming flowers to freshly cut grass, each aroma sent his senses reeling. With eager steps, Bali loped through the streets, stopping at every bush and streetlight pole to fill his nostrils with new fragrances and mark his presence on the territory. After covering several blocks, he finally slowed to a walk, his head spinning from the overwhelming mix of scents. Suddenly, a squirrel scolded him from a nearby tree; despite the challenge, Bali didn't feel any anger toward them anymore. Instead, he barked happily in response.

This was the life he had always longed for—filled with the thrill of adventure and endless possibilities waiting to be explored. His heart beat excitedly as he set foot onto the uncharted path ahead, filled with anticipation and a burning desire to discover new places and experience new things. This was the life he had dreamed of, where each day brought a new journey, and every step held the potential for something extraordinary.

As he turned a corner, he nearly ran into a cat napping lazily in a driveway. The cat was lying curled up in the warm sun, his fur a mix of black and white patches, each overshadowing the sunlight differently. Slit and golden, his eyes blinked contentedly as it dozed. This cat still hissed at him, but Bali didn't let it faze him. He barked a friendly greeting and continued his journey, undeterred by anything in his path. Nothing could dampen his spirits in this moment of pure freedom and joy.

Bali Back to The Road

The bustling New York City bullet train station was a sea of people during the hectic Friday morning rush hour. Amid the chaos, four figures slinked through the crowds, their movements calculated as they tried to avoid being recorded by security cameras and drones—remaining anonymous was crucial in their line of work. Fortunately, the face recognition system was almost impossible to maintain and update because of its terrible reputation among the youngest of the population. The young people decided to cover their faces as soon as they were in public. This reaction to the government's invasion of privacy began in late 2040. These actions blocked its full implementation, contrary to what happened in Asia during the first two decades of the twenty-first century.

Besides, this system recently faced a significant shift with the enactment of the Americas Union Treaty in September 2050—an agreement among the countries in the American continent(s). This marketing measure was implemented to boost the trade of US products across the continent. Thus, many people were moving in and out of the United States for business opportunities. States such as California and New York witnessed a significant influx of entrepreneurs and business owners, which hadn't been seen in a while. As expected, our quartet was aware of this weakness in the security system and took all the advantages it would provide them.

Still, our four jokers tried not to attract any attention. They also avoided using the new ultra-durable disposable paper clothes that were so fashionable and decided instead to use ultra-conservative clothes. In this sense, their dress code was casual yet intelligent attire to blend in with the vast of other travelers. Besides, they all, male or female, were wearing their light winter coats and pants, shielding them from the occasional chilly winter air. However, do not let their looks swindle you; these amigos also use them to pack valuable objects. They were here not for a leisurely trip; they were petty thieves on a mission.

Despite being four people, they had only purchased two tickets online for this journey. And even those tickets were not entirely legitimate. They had a computer-smart boss who knew how to maneuver the network to get access to discounts he was not entitled to. Also, he discreetly installed an application on their cellphone that could mimic a ticket to pass by the train's electronic ticket scanner. This would allow them to emulate one extra boarding pass from the one they got at a not-face price. The boss knew that trying to get extra duplicates may not be effective, as they had already tried that before. So, it was a risky move, but they would take the chance to circumvent the scanning system that guarded the entrance to the bullet train bound for Toronto, Canada. The boss always said: "To make a good profit, one always has to reduce costs." The thrill of the risk was palpable in the air.

The High Administration at the National Railroad Passenger Corporation, doing business as Amtrak, introduced the mandatory 'Quick Response' or QR scanning system at the end of 2030, believing it would prevent fraud, a significant threat to the train's finances. Additionally, to discourage temptations, a person traveling without a ticket would be obliged to pay the full single fare or full return fare and a stiff penalty fare for the journey of two thousand dollars. However, these cunning thieves had found a way around it by mimicking tickets and, when trapped, blaming the seller if they could convince the authorities. Using their tech skills to outsmart the system was a feat that would impress the most seasoned cyber experts. Their cunning was a testament to their cyber-intelligence and resourcefulness.

As they approached the security turnstiles, one of the thieves maintained a facade of calmness, his genuine fear hidden deep within. His outward appearance gave nothing away about the turmoil in his mind. He was scared to his core, his heart pounding in his chest, although he couldn't let that show—not now.

Under their meticulous plan, the group kept their distance from each other as they moved toward their target—six feet apart, to be exact—adhering to social distancing guidelines created at the end of 2019 to prevent the spread of the coronavirus. Their eyes darted around nervously, only tracking each other through subtle glances and slight movements.

With bated breath and nerves on edge, they continued forward toward their goal: to board the bullet train without getting caught and make their journey to Canada as planned. With a cool facade that betrayed the adrenaline coursing through his veins, the thief leading the group approached the turnstile first. His heart pounded in his chest like a drum, and each beat echoed in his ears as he swiped his phone over the scanner. A split second of dread washed over him as he waited for the system to detect the mimicked ticket. Much to his relief, the light turned green, indicating his boarding was approved.

The one they called 'number one' of the bandits, hand shook violently as he passed through the QR access control, his nerves on edge as he tried to maintain calm. The second in command followed smoothly with his so-called 'regular ticket,' with a smug grin as he breezed through without issue. However, as the third member of their gang tried to use the fake app on his cell phone, a bright red light filled this particular boarding line at the station, and an alarm pierced the air in that embarkment area.

As the brigands realized their plan was unraveling, a tsunami of panic engulfed them. The thought of their last two fellows being caught and their fraudulent tickets exposed sent shockwaves of fear through their bodies. The security guard, a formidable figure, appeared before the scoundrel, his presence a stark reminder of their impending doom. Beads of sweat formed on their foreheads as they exchanged nervous glances, fully aware of the dire consequences if their scheme was discovered.

"Sir, there seems to be a problem here," the security guard calmly explained with a firm, no-nonsense voice.

The bandit swallowed hard, trying to muster his confidence as he shook his head. "No, no problem at all. Just a little mix-up with the app. You know how technology can be," he said nervously.

The security guard narrowed his eyes and said, "Let the Security Officer look at your ticket. If everything is in order, you will leave here on the next train."

"Of course, let's see your boss," he said, trying to keep his cool.

In a desperate bid, the last bandit hurried forward with his quasi-authentic ticket, his heart racing with fear. It was the ticket from which they had copied the one that set off the alarm. He passed through by some stroke of luck, and a wave of overwhelming relief washed over the petty criminals. They fled the scene, their meticulously planned heist almost torn down, yet at least they had escaped the first immediate danger.

The ultra shimmer of the sun blared their movements as the three cunning outlaws made their way onto the sleek bullet train. Each held tightly to their own dark motives and twisted schemes; together, a common goal bound them. The youngest of the trio shifted uncomfortably in his seat, his nerves on edge in this new world of misdeeds and deceptions. Still, his desire for financial freedom was more substantial than any hesitation he may have felt, driving him to join forces with the other three seasoned criminals, known for their daring heists and fearless tactics.

Another clan member, an unlawful young missy without a designated seat or ticket, was swinging car to car, evading vigilant ticket inspectors and blending in with the innocent passengers to conduct her business. She precisely calculated her movements as she weaved through the crowded train. Her green eyes darted back and forth in search of any potential threats or prey. Together, these three unlikely colleagues traveled toward their ultimate destination, ready to carry out their carefully crafted plans and emerge victorious in their lawless pursuits.

The sleek and high-tech design of the bullet train provided the perfect clientele for her thievery, allowing her and the others to seamlessly snatch small valuables like credit cards, jewelry, and watches from unsuspecting travelers. With only two planned stops on the route—one before crossing the border into Canada and the other at its ultimate destination of Toronto—they all had limited time to execute this portion of their plan. Racing at breakneck speeds of nearly 330 miles (531.10 kilometers) per hour, the journey would last barely one hour and 30 minutes. Then, the time needed to clear customs added only another 40 minutes thanks to advanced technology. This brings the total time to approximately two hours and ten minutes, depending on weather conditions.

However, luck took a cruel turn for this pickpocket young woman when she attempted to swipe a wallet from a seated passenger, only to be discovered by an undercover FBI agent posing as a vacationer in the adjacent seat. Her movements were exposed through a reflection in the window, revealing her malicious activities and sealing her inevitable downfall.

The thief's heart raced in her chest as she desperately sought a way to flee once she realized she had been discovered. She wasn't entirely sure, but her feminine instinct had never let her down, and this wouldn't be the first time. Then she remembered a soft voice whispering in her ears: "You must escape quickly."

Thinking she was clever, she was caught off guard soon after a stout blond woman suddenly rose from her seat and sought to intercept her. As she attempted to make her way to the next car with the stolen wallet still in hand, she couldn't shake the feeling that she was being observed. And just as she reached for the door, a firm hand seized her shoulder.

She turned to see the cold and determined gaze of a female FBI agent staring back at her. To her surprise, the agent's expression wasn't one of anger or disgust instead of amusement. This blonde athletic agent, almost six feet tall and with a robust build, nearly couldn't contain her laughter as she thought that of all those on the train, she would never have suspected this baby-faced lady could be a pickpocket.

"You thought you could outsmart us," the agent said with a smirk, snatching the wallet from the thief's grasp. The thief felt conflicted—maybe relieved she was to get caught before she could get away but also frustrated because she had failed to outwit the authorities. She could feel the threat of tears welling up in her eyes as she realized that a potential conviction could result in a year-long prison sentence.

As the bullet train raced through the towns of New York, the two remaining rascals kept a close eye on their pal, who was being escorted by a security agent with handcuffs this time, for a change. They remained calmly in their seats, not reacting as they scanned their surroundings. With a quick, furtive glance around, they caught sight of the guards stationed at the end of the carriage, their eyes always watchful.

They seemed to say to each other with an impatient glance. "Relax, the train is heavily guarded, so let's not do anything rash." They both couldn't avoid feeling the tension crackling in the air like static electricity. The youngest's fingers, who seemed ready to play a piano concert, remained hidden in his pockets while his hands were shaking.

As they neared the border between Canada and the United States, the oldest member of the pair felt a twinge of anxiety. Memories of past struggles with strict security measures flooded his mind. However, this time, luck was on their side; all of their documents were in order, and the inspection was passed with no incidents.

The historic Amtrak train station in Toronto, Canada, was bustling with activity as the Maple Leaf company continued to operate it with exceptional services to their distinguished customers. The shrill blast of a whistle pierced the air, signaling the approach of a train. Our two incidental friends clung tightly to their backpacks, an unspoken understanding as they checked for any unattended valuables by questionable means while passing through all the other passengers. At the end of their trip, they were content with their journey as the train provided them with a relatively smooth ride and good clientele despite a few bumps along the way.

As the oldest thief stepped off the train first at their destination, a sudden flash in his face caught his attention. "What is this?" he muttered to himself before answering with a resigned sigh, "Another extra security measure... They never stop improving." Then, they both navigated through the enlarged waiting area and onto a platform designated for wheelchair access, deftly avoiding the crowds as they made their way to the parking lot, where they planned to steal a car. Time was of the essence, and now they need to keep the momentum moving ahead.

As they reached the parking lot, a sleek electric vehicle descended from the sky and landed nearby. One passenger came out of the flying limousine with a big poster that read: "Marsha Ponzi." A couple of minutes later, a stylish young woman with a Corgi on a leash approached the gentleman in the vehicle. The elder of the two amigos, called 'Ben,' was able to hear part of the conversation when the driver approached her: "Miss Marcha, there was a change of plans, and Dr. Locus wants you and Bali to go immediately to the station two as the principal one got destroyed."

For the petty thieves, there was no time to lose; they had a mission and quotas to meet. Yet, the old burglar couldn't resist looking at the Corgi with a friendly face, and he radiated joy in his eyes. Ben firmly believed he had heard the puppy say *"good morning"* to him. He also couldn't avoid noticing the puppy's blue left eye. Ben thought that the Corgi-puppy was, maybe, a little less than a year old, judging by his appearance. It was a beautiful Corgi with a golden face and light fawn body, part of his loin and back of a gorgeous dark black color of "vantablack," highlighting the snow white of his paws and the end of the small tail.

At the parking lot, the old man (as his partner amicably had nicknamed Ben) was trying to hot-wire an electric, utterly autonomous car. In contrast, his partner looked in awe at a cutting-edge hydrogen flying vehicle. "Hey, old man, this must cost a fortune," he said quietly (but with an expression of astonishment) to his partner Ben, a weathered-looking man in his late 30s due to his tumultuous past. He called him "old man" in a loving and affectionate way due to the degree of friendship that had grown between them. Ben didn't feel offended, nor did Renato Grace, at being called Ginger. The last one was still single and had his youth on his side. Ben had already been married twice and had a daughter with his second wife. He had always kept his factual occupation a secret from his family, telling his wife and daughter that he worked as an independent installer of home alarm systems.

"Can you drive one of those?" asked Ben, but his red-haired accomplice shook his head. Undeterred, they continued their plan to steal a car—an essential part of their lawless operations in the city—and time was already ticking. The entire terminal and parking lot security system monitored time, movements, conversations, and actions through microphones, cameras, drones, and the support of androids specially designed for these purposes. They knew that they had to move fast to be successful.

Luckily for them, some resources had been cut due to budget constraints, and only the instruments remained on display to discourage those with no good intentions. Somehow, the old man's experience allowed him to permeate those small details, and he knew how to take advantage of these weaknesses of the security system.

As one rustler fumbled with the door lock of a 2039 hybrid car, a sleek and modern vehicle that ran on a mix of gasoline and electricity, his partner attempted to disable the safety systems of another completely autonomous electric vehicle. Their first attempts were in vain. The first criminal lacked the necessary knowledge and experience with the advanced technology of the 2030s. At the same time, the other was no match for the sophisticated defense mechanisms that protected vehicles beyond the year 2047.

Suddenly, a bright orange light illuminated the parking lot where they stood, casting an eerie glow over their unlawful activities. The operational security cameras were equipped with state-of-the-art technology, immediately detected abnormal behavior in their sector, and activated an alarm system. Within minutes, a low rumbling sound could be heard in the distance, drawing closer and closer with each passing moment. It was the sound of a robotic android stealthily advancing toward them from the south. The android was tall and sleek, its outer frame gleaming in the pale orange light of the parking lot. He moved with precise and fluid movements, his clothing illuminated by the flashing lights of the security cameras.

As if that wasn't enough trouble, security drones were almost there to swarm above them with more security cameras. Their powerful lights scanned every inch of the scene below as they moved closer. The bandits were lucky that day—the interactive security cameras were offline for maintenance, providing enough time to leave the area undetected, unrecorded, and unidentified. This incident served as a reminder of how technology can be both a blessing and a curse—beautiful when it benefits us and disastrous when it fails us.

The two pilferers felt a shiver race through them as they realized the security system might have discovered them. Still, they were prepared for this moment, and without hesitation, each took off in a different direction. They moved swiftly yet calmly, avoiding suspicion as they weaved through the rows of parked cars in the lot. Whenever an alarm went off, or security drones approached, they seamlessly blended in with other people, casually asking for directions or the time. That was why they selected a busy day at the station.

They continued their calculated dance for over ten minutes, walking in opposite directions and occasionally doubling back as if searching for their vehicles. The older of the two had a determined look on his face as he pulled out an ultra-small laptop and began hacking into the system of a nearby semi-autonomous electric vehicle. His partner watched from a safe distance, a small smile playing on his lips despite the beads of sweat that dotted his forehead. It was all part of the thrill for him.

As the car's engine roared to life and they made their escape, adrenaline rushed through their veins. The semi-autonomous electric vehicle was sleek and futuristic, with a streamlined design that seamlessly blended into the surroundings. Its shiny exterior reflected the parking lot's lights, and the tinted windows hid the state-of-the-art technology inside. Having been able to hack the vehicle's security system successfully helped them complete another heist, leaving behind a trail of confusion and chaos in their wake. They didn't even think of the owner's horror when he or she discovered someone else was now driving the stolen automobile. Yet, time was of the essence here, as the stolen vehicle's internal computer, which had not easy access, could soon start its own trick. Once activated by the owner, it would transmit its location and send a message to the police.

Although the car appeared smooth and almost glass-like, running a hand over the surface revealed a subtle texture, like tiny grooves etched across the body to ensure its resistance and easy destruction into small fragments, less likely to cause harm to humans in an accident. The handle of the car door was cool to the touch, and once inside, the seats were surprisingly soft and cushioned. As they drove away to the city, both knew that this was the beginning of another chapter in their daring lives as professional petty thieves.

Twenty miles apart, Bali was trotting slowly through the desolate streets of the suburb of the affluents, his footsteps echoing off the perfectly manicured sidewalks. Each step felt heavy, as if he were carrying a weight on his shoulders. The once serene and pristine neighborhood now seemed foreign and unfamiliar to him, causing his heart to race like a trapped bird frantically trying to escape his now open cage. There was nothing but emptiness and silence everywhere he turned—no signs of life or guidance.

As he continued on, lost and unsure of his next move, a sudden screech of brakes caught his attention. A young boy on a bicycle in vibrant green, with a frame gleaming in the sunlight as it glided through the streets. The wheels' spokes spun hypnotically, creating a blur of silver and chrome. He appeared out of nowhere, bringing with him the energy and vibrancy that had been missing from the neighborhood until now.

He was a flash of youth and adventure, his bright eyes and mischievous smile a beacon of hope in this otherwise desolate neighborhood. His bicycle was his chariot, and his backpack engraved with the name 'Lucas' symbolized his independence and fearlessness. There was a sense of destiny swirling around him as if he was meant to change the course of this forgotten street.

Lucas was confidently pedaling through the streets of Bali's neighborhood. At only fourteen years old, he was already familiar with every nook and cranny of this neighborhood, finding comfort in its security and calmness. He could navigate through the following fourteen blocks south or the other eight north blindfolded. This was his favorite place to ride his bike because it made him feel secure, and he couldn't resist the beauty surrounding him. However, today, something new caught his attention amid the usual routine: a lost puppy he was determined to find and possibly keep as his own.

Despite all his perceived intelligence and cleverness, Lucas had underestimated Bali's agility and determination. In this cat-and-mouse game, the little puppy with short legs proved to be a challenge for the overconfident boy on his bike. As they both weaved through the immaculate streets, Bali's determination to elude capture grew stronger with each passing moment. This once peaceful neighborhood now held an exhilarating sense of adventure for Bali, one that he had never experienced before in his sheltered upbringing.

Despite the adrenaline coursing through him, Bali remained calm and calculating. He darted across the intersection with sleek, agile movements, disappearing into the thick bushes that lined the front yard of a nearby house. The determined young man chasing after him quickly dismounted his bike and gave chase on foot. Bali was always one step ahead, using his keen ability to hide among the overgrown shrubbery in front of another house.

Lucas refused to give up and got on his bike again as the stretch became longer with each run. He was determined to catch his mischievous target. Slowly, he followed Bali's trail through the dense foliage, pushing branches and leaves aside as he went. However, no matter how close Lucas thought he was getting, Bali seemed to effortlessly slip away, leading him on a wild goose chase throughout the neighborhood.

Finally, after a series of twists and turns, Lucas managed to close in on Bali. With a burst of energy and a playful leap, Bali eluded his grasp once again, sprinting out into the open garden of the following nearby house as the front fence swung open. Despite the frustration of being so close yet so far from catching his elusive quarry, Lucas couldn't avoid admiring Bali's cleverness and speed.

"How lucky that little dog is!" Lucas shouted, his voice echoing off the walls of the house nearby. He couldn't believe it. He couldn't imagine the audacity of that innocent-looking dog. "How could he reason and plan to evade my premeditated and calculating reasoning?" This challenge got his adrenaline pumping, and now it was becoming personal.

Despite his frustration, he wasn't ready to stop yet. Determined, he hopped on his bike once again and pedaled furiously, weaving through the next house, passing the one he spotted Bali on, hoping to catch him on the front side of the house as Bali was running out of air and soon would need to rest—even for a little. As he waited at the front end of that house, Lucas rummaged through his backpack and found an uneaten chicken sandwich with melted cheese.

With a flicker of excitement, he hatched a brilliant plan to use the sandwich as a bait. The crispy, golden melted cheese oozing out of the sandwich were sure to lure in his unsuspecting victim. However, conscious that too much cheese is not good for dogs he decided to take part of it out. Still the chicken still smell savory. His mouth watering at the smell of the snack, he carefully unwrapped the sandwich, getting it right to entice his target. He couldn't wait to see the success of his clever scheme unfold.

Carefully placing each foot on the crunchy leaves and avoiding the twigs, Lucas made his way to the bushes in the front fence at almost the middle of the house's front yard, where the entrance door was half open. He was sitting in expectation and tuning his ears. He knew Bali would not pass up the opportunity to exit through an open gate. Bali indeed knew the secret of how to sneak through the gaps between the ground and the bottom of the fence because of small landslides. Yet, between having to dig and move an open gate, he was confident that Bali would opt for the latter option.

Lucas believed he could hear Bali's excited barks in the distance, signaling he was running to the front of the house to find a way out. With determination, Lucas spotted the small entrance door and made sure it was a bit open, and part of his sandwich was waiting for him right there. He quickly ducked behind the little bushes near a hedge of flowers in the front of the house. The prickly leaves scratched at his face as he waited patiently, ignoring the itchiness. A rustle in the grass caught his attention, and he held his breath while waiting for Bali to appear.

So, Bali flagrantly came out as expected through the open entrance door near the bushes in the middle of the house's fence. Sitting quietly on the grass, Lucas slowly reached out his hand with another piece of sandwich. The plan was to gain his trust. Also, as he predicted, Bali stopped to catch his breath. Then, he seemed to smell the chicken and looked curiously at the offer. He sniffed the food before him, timidly approaching it. Lucas smiled when the puppy began to trust him, a heartwarming moment that brought a smile to his face. With delicate care, he quickly took Bali and hugged him in his arms without sudden movement after he finished the other piece of sandwich.

Lucas expertly balanced the weight of his new doggy in his left arm while controlling the handlebars of his bike with his right hand. He didn't want to put him in his front basket, fearing that he might jump from there to the ground. The wheels hummed against the pavement as he rode along, pedaling down a winding side street parallel to the main road. The scent of freshly cut grass and blooming flowers filled the air, a pleasant contrast to the dusty exhaust fumes of the main road as there were, until now, a lot of vehicles burning fuels like gasoline, gas, and ethanol.

"Just a little longer to get home," Lucas thought. His home was on the outskirts of an affluent residential area, a neighborhood primarily of professionals and their families. While the houses were well-maintained, they lacked the grandeur and opulence of those owned by the wealthiest.

These homes were more modest in design, with simpler facades and less elaborate decorations. Even so, they continued to exude an air of elegance and wealth. As Lucas approached his house, he couldn't avert feeling grateful for the comfortable life his parents had built for them in this middle-class community. His mother luckily got a better job with better pay after his father passed away, and although they barely kept their assets afloat, they safeguarded their lifestyle.

As Lucas returned home and stepped through the front door, he was met with a barrage of questions from his mother, who immediately noticed the small, trembling puppy cradled in his arms. Her voice was a quilt of tones, soft and soothing, though, with an underlying edge that could slice through the fabric of lies. And now, as she looked at her son, her eyes held a mix of concern and love, her maternal instincts fiercely protecting and nurturing. Despite her emotions, her intellect clearly told her that keeping this animal was not financially plausible at this time.

"Where did you get that puppy?" she demanded, her tone sharp and disapproving. Lucas braced himself for her scolding as he explained how he had found him wandering alone on the streets. His mother's face softened at the mention of the abandoned dog, but she insisted he take it back to where he found him. However, Lucas's determined gaze held steady as he refused to return this helpless creature back to the road.

Lucas begged his mother to understand his motives with pleading eyes and a quiver in his voice. "This little dog was all alone and lost. I can't abandon him now," he pleaded.

His mother sighed resignedly, knowing her son's compassion could not be swayed. She relented and suggested they go to the small row of shops about twelve blocks east of their house. Maybe they could find someone there who would take him, or perhaps someone would recognize him and return him to his rightful home.

A boiling mix of fury and despair consumed Lucas, his hands trembling as he clenched them into fists. "Why does nothing ever work out for me?" he roared, the sound echoing off the walls with a raw intensity. "My father would have understood. He would have let me keep the doggy!" yet deep down, Lucas knew it was a lie. His father had always held firm to the rules, and his mother knew. The memories flooded back of how his father had always been on her side, never genuinely seeing or hearing him.

Lucas stormed around the room with a growl of frustration, knocking over furniture and sending cherished family heirlooms crashing to the ground in a destructive display. As he tripped over the entrance table, shattering the delicate vase that had been passed down for generations, Lucas felt his control slipping away, along with any hope of resolution. When the vase fell, his grandmother's voice could be heard telling him: "Take care of your mother, my dear child."

The sharp fragments of glass gleamed mockingly, as did the cruel reflection of the chaos unfolding. Lucas was caught between seething anger and crippling fear, his emotions swirling like a violent storm within him. He knew his mother's rage would be fierce; even so, what he feared most was her profound disappointment in him. As Lucas braced himself for the coming storm, the room felt heavy, weighed down by tension and shattered dreams.

"Why did you do that?" his mother's voice cut through the air like a sharpened blade. It didn't matter that she had scolded him hard; Lucas could see the fire of rage brewing behind her eyes. "With your university coming up, we can't afford any extra expenses," she spat out with venomous disdain.

Heartbroken and angry, Lucas clenches his fists until his nails dig into his palms, a physical manifestation of the pain and helplessness he felt. He knew he had to let go of his new canine friend, a pure and innocent bond ripped away by the cruel twist of fate. It was an unfair burden he must bear, a bitter pill he was forced to swallow. All he could do at that moment was to grit his teeth and accept it, with tears stinging his eyes and a lump lodged in his throat.

The sting of tears pricked at his eyes, but he forced them back with a fierce determination and bolted to his room. He left this brief canine companion behind as a symbol of surrender, knowing he couldn't protect him. Bali's silence was deafening, starkly contrasting to his usual cheerful barks. Lucas was no stranger to disappointment and sacrifice, even at the tender age of fourteen. Although, this time, it felt like a crushing weight on his shoulders, threatening to break him. Yet another hurdle to conquer in his life.

Lucas ascended to his room on the second level of the residence and immediately headed toward his mother's bedroom. From the front window, he could see the driveway of their home. He wanted to catch another glimpse of that little dog's face so he wouldn't forget him; perhaps he would reencounter him on the streets. "What will I do if I come across him again?" Lucas pondered with a tinge of nostalgia and helplessness, knowing there was nothing he could have done differently. However, that was something to be addressed at a later time.

Lucas's mother spoke the commands to the interactive voice system in her semi-autonomous vehicle. She sank into her seat and took a deep breath—one that Lucas could feel through the cracks in the old windows as the air flowed out of the house. They needed to be replaced, yet their finances were tight at the moment. With bittersweetness, Lucas watched as his little companion disappeared into the horizon. His mother's car glided smoothly south toward the teeming business plaza about twelve blocks away from their residence.

Bali Found a Friend

After hot-wiring another vehicle since leaving the train station, this time a flashy, un-autonomous sports car, the two cunning thieves cruised through the bustling streets of downtown Toronto until they reached a luxurious five-star hotel. The valet attendant took their keys, praising their set of wheels as they strutted into the lobby, pretending to be wealthy guests. They were wearing their disposable copies of trendy clothes in Ruff-N-Tuff paper to make them look like knock-off originals of famous designer brands. They were almost indistinguishable from the real thing. So, as they checked in, they marveled at the opulence surrounding them, feeling like kings in their own kingdom.

In their room, they indulged in a lavish bubble bath and feasted on gourmet food ordered from room service, all charged to a stolen credit card hidden inside their cell phone's SD memory cards. It was a very outdated technology, yet its resourcefulness made it a perfect cover. Once again, time was of the essence, and they could not risk being caught by staying too long in one place. They quickly dressed in casual clothes with light winter jackets and prepared for their next heist, stealing from high-end stores in the prestigious downtown mall or robbing their clientele to resell the valuables later in New York City.

After enjoying their refreshing baths, they left the room and walked to the parking lot when a bellboy from the hotel began chasing them. They didn't know whether to run or confront the young man, but they listened to what he had to say since he came alone. "Well, gentlemen, the parking valet found your fancy Breguet Classique Tourbillon watch."

"Oh, thank you so much! Please tell the person who found it that he can charge his lunch today to our room — whatever he wants to eat." With no further delays, they went out to continue their misdeeds.

Later, during their lawless activities in a pre-selected store, one of the security agents recognized one of them from a previous robbery eleven months ago. This security guard, with a memory as sharp as a knife, still remembered the face of this suspect. Unaware of the security agent's actions, the young-at-heart, and his partner in crimes, the red-haired man continued their misdeeds, slowly filling the extra pockets added in layers to their light winter jackets with valuables and chuckling at the thrill of danger.

A robbery report in another store crackled on the guard's radio at the precise moment when he wanted to identify this suspect. As duty commands, he immediately rushed to the central office of security agents. Thus, after collaborating on their task, he reported the situation at his store to his superior about 45 minutes later. Perhaps they could join forces to catch this petty criminal. Unfortunately, he got no group collaboration, and there was merely one extra body to join him in a few minutes—if still available.

As he prepared to confront the thief or thieves, the guard felt fear creeping up his spine. He knew the situation could worsen and longed for more support. Sooner or later, he'll have to protect his store, even alone, because the mall lacks security officers. Thus, he urgently navigated the building's corridors with only one backup on his way and adrenaline pumping. This suspect had already escaped once, adding to the tension of a potential confrontation. Now, the game of cat and mouse was about to start, and he felt the weight of responsibility on his shoulders.

Finally, the other guard joined him, and as they approached the jewelry store, where suspicious activity was in progress, every instinct urged him to call for more backups. His hand tightened around his radio, ready to call for more help at any moment. Swiftly, the voice crackled through: "Suspects have fled the scene." The guard's heart sank as he wondered where their target could have disappeared. They couldn't afford to let him slip away again. The mind of the store guard raced as he strategized their next move, determined to stay one step ahead of the elusive lawbreaker.

Panic set in for the two rascals as they noticed the two guards approaching and one communicating their location through his portable radio. They realized their activities had been compromised and knew they had no time to waste. They moved fast into the food court next to the jewelry store. Darting between tables in a low crouch, they used their tried-and-true escape technique to make their way to the back of the food court to get into the restaurant located in the corner of the mall.

Despite their haste, the two amigos couldn't shake the fear and uncertainty that weighed heavily on their hearts. "Will this be the time I finally get caught?" the oldest thought. When they reached the end of the corridor, they slid behind the doors, entered the kitchen, and tried blending in with their bustling activities. Ben wondered whether to hide the valuables somewhere to avoid being caught flagrantly. Maybe they could retrieve them later, once nothing could be proven against them.

The security guards were required to wear black pants and light blue shirts as uniforms with their mall cellphones for better identification and communication. This also made them easy to identify by their criminal counterparts. As they cautiously approached the locked restaurant's side door, their foreheads were sweaty, and their hands shook as they searched for the lock assigned to the security agents. Their hearts beat with a mixture of confidence and fear. They monitored all the surrounding movements to avoid missing the slightest detail because they were unsure where the suspect or suspects had gone.

The two partners in crime had entered the kitchen about nine minutes earlier, enough time to plan their escape. Upon entering, they kept their faces expressionless, not looking at anybody's eyes, and their movements controlled as they made their way through. They quickly put on white gowns and disposable bouffant caps, those the prep cooks used to cover their heads. This way, they blended in with the busy staff working in the kitchen. That day, they were working on a special order for the senator of that congressional district that would take place in about 30 minutes at that restaurant, located at the corner of the food court with the main entrance facing the parking lot.

Since people constantly came in and out, some taking out cardboard boxes because of the preparation for that day's special event, our friend Ben saw a fascinating escape option. "Follow my steps. Copy everything I do," Ben said to Ginger, emphasizing their unity.

They loaded up some empty boxes, and with them on their shoulders, they navigated through the maze of hot stoves and damp shelves used for meal preparation before finally reaching the trash bins at the back of the kitchen. Every second seemed like an eternity as they prayed to avoid unwanted attention before exiting through the back door. When they finally entered the small final alley that led to the building's exit, it seemed like a death trap. They knew that the security guards could appear at any time.

Every bump from a passing employee sent shivers down their spines. "Where are you two going?" one cook asked.

"We are pitching in to clear the clutter because it has become unmanageable," Ben replied with a clever remark.

"Go! Hurry up and then assist with the preparations. The banquet starts at any moment, and we need all hands-on deck," the cook said.

They got scared, yet a small part of them reveled in the chase's thrill and adrenaline rush. It was a conflicting mix of emotions as they carried out their devious plan, torn between fear and excitement. They finally arrived at the dumpsters and hovered there for about an hour or a little more.

When the thugs were going to leave the dumpsters, a sudden rush of people poured out of the restaurant's banquet; some doubled over and wretched into the parking lot. It was like a scene from a comedy movie, with mass food poisoning striking all at once. A few reached nearby garbage cans before vomiting, but most were left spewing up, gasping for air, and grasping their stomachs in agony. The wail of police sirens echoed through the area, followed by the hydrogen-powered Zeppelins ambulances coming to the rescue.

Also, the senator's electric helicopter, equipped with dual rotors and fans, lifted off into the sky. With their faces now smeared with coal ash for disguise, the young thugs emerged from the mall's garbage disposals on the east side.

"Someone clearly attempted to pull a cruel prank on the Senator," the younger man said.

Little did they know that the senator became the Canadian president some years later. The oldest man grinned slyly at the young man, and they tossed their cooking hats. They quickly discarded their stolen white chef gowns, too, and began scouring the area for an escape plan, their minds working overtime.

They constantly changed cars and lodgings to avoid leaving traces of their presence. It made sense for them to search for a new vehicle instead of trying to find the previous one. Sometimes, they move in opposite directions to their destination to avoid leaving a trace and then take an Uber or bus to the final destination.

With his experience with semi-autonomous cars, Ben quickly hijacked a similar vehicle without incident. In no time, they were speeding away in the sleek electric vehicle, their clever plan unfolding—at last. The engine's sound hummed beneath them as they weaved through traffic, their adrenaline coursing through their veins.

"It would be best not to return to this shopping center again," the youngest proposed as he finally returned to his usual mien—this impressive escape continued to revolve in his head.

It was a difficult time, and despite having emerged triumphant, they questioned whether it was still worth continuing that life of crime or if it was time to find an honest way of living, even if it paid little money. Yet, they weren't ready to give up the thrill of their adventurous life just yet. The aged one glanced at his partner, their faces illuminated by the flickering lights of the moving traffic as daylight started dwindling. The recent heist had been a close call, and now doubts lingered like a heavy fog.

"Tring… Tring… Tring!" The old cellphone phone rang.

"How's everything going, Ben?" a young woman's voice asked on the other end of the connection.

"All is going well, baby! I'll be back in town in a couple of days," he said.

"How's the business convention going in Toronto?" she asked.

"The organizers welcomed us as soon as we arrived, and the activities went as planned. The convention is going fantastic."

Because of the distracting conversation with the young woman, the driver crashed into the car in front of him a few feet (meters) later, jolting them forward and causing their hearts to race again. The stolen vehicle offered no protection with its deactivated security system, as the driver impaired it when he stole it, leaving it vulnerable to the impact.

The once sturdy car now crumpled like a tin can, and its alarms blared uselessly. Ben regretted getting distracted as he realized his poor judgment had put them in a dangerous and precarious situation, which they now desperately had to escape.

"What happened? What was that sound?" the young lady at the other end of the line asked.

"Nothing, baby. A waitress at the convention dropped all the dishes on her tray, and the other one behind her slipped, and they both fell. I think I'm going to help them. I'll contact you later, my love," he hastily spoke into his phone before ending the call with a kiss.

The urgency in his voice was palpable as they quickly exited the damaged car and made a beeline for the nearest sidewalk. They barely glanced at the other driver, who would most likely demand to exchange insurance information. Their chief concern was getting away before anyone could catch on to their illegal activities.

Their hearts pounded in their chests, adrenaline coursing through their bodies again as they hastily exited the car. They scanned their surroundings with panicked eyes, desperately searching for an escape route. Honking cars and busy pedestrians overwhelmed them on the bustling street. Even though they focused on the approaching bus at the next intersection, its bright red "B" sign stood out against the only cloud in the sky in the distance.

"There are no drones yet, which is a weird situation in a city controlled by AI," the older thought.

They sprinted toward the bus stop without hesitation, their feet pounding against the pavement. The smell of exhaust fumes and damp concrete filled the air, mixed with the scent of fear and desperation as they hurried to catch their next ride.

Every second felt like an eternity as they tried to remain inconspicuous and make it to the bus before it departed. The fear of being caught by the android-controlled transportation added to their urgency; they knew there would be no mercy or second chances. As they walked quickly, their frantic breaths echoed in the chaos, but they couldn't afford to slow down. This was their better chance at survival in this dystopian world where humans were mere pawns in a game controlled more and more by computers.

Finally, they reached the bus and boarded it before the automated system closed the doors behind them. Breathing heavily, they dared not look back at the chaos they left behind at the accident scene. The oldest thief sat near the front; his red-haired companion opted for the back to avoid attracting suspicion. The tension between them was palpable as they remained silent for almost 40 minutes, still reeling from their daring escape.

As the eldest's eyes scanned the luxurious houses lining the street, a feeling of greed and excitement washed over him. He couldn't resist the temptation of the wealthy homes, each like a treasure chest waiting to be opened. As he gazed at his friend, a feeling of unease began to emerge.

The young man shifted nervously and voiced his doubts about the plan from the distance. "I don't know, old man," he muttered under his breath. "Maybe we should lie low for a little while."

His old friend couldn't overlook the excitement of the possibility of riches. Ben approached him as he had already decided to take action; it was clear by the mischievous grin on his face. "Don't let fear take over, man," he softly said, striving to remain indomitable. The bus got to a stop, and they gathered together in the back. "We didn't come all this way to turn back now. Think about what we could find inside those homes." Deep down, the old man knew some of him wanted to heed his inside warning, but he couldn't deny the pull toward adventure and freedom that tugged at his heart.

As they strolled past a bustling shopping plaza and entered a wealthy neighborhood, their minds brimmed with ideas for their subsequent thievery. They eyed the lavish homes and manicured lawns, wondering what treasures lay waiting inside. The thrill of their criminal deeds pulsed through their veins, a rush of adrenaline that never failed to excite them. The unknown possibilities ahead beckoned them further down the path of brazen lawlessness. These emotions and feelings were like a drug, pulling them deeper into a life of daring heists and forbidden thrills.

— — —

Back to the Hashbuns residence.

"Bali, come on! It's time to eat!" shouted his owner, who had not yet noticed his departure. The sun was again setting over the tranquil suburban neighborhood of the Hashbun, and Bali had slipped out of his owner's yard once more. His owners, preoccupied with their lives, didn't notice his departure until it was time to prepare Bali's dinner. Not for nothing, Bali has been feeling lonely lately. No one was giving him real attention. He was not a lousy doggy; he had a brief moment of fury while pursuing the cat, Zizzo. Bali had it very clear in his mind that the destruction of the sofa was all his fault.

Neither Tatiana nor the lady who helped with the cleaning or her daughter after returning from the university noticed his departure. Because the Hashbuns had been paying for training to settle Bali down for months, they thought it might finally be paying off. Tatiana called out for him, searching among the tall oaks and bushes that lined the fence on the west side of their property. She went to the end of the backyard, too. Yet, Bali was nowhere to be found.

Panic set in as she frantically searched every corner of their yard—under the terrace where he liked to nap and among the bushes where he loved to play with butterflies. Still, there was no sign of Bali. Her heart filled with sorrow and anguish at the thought of her beloved pet being gone. She immediately notified her daughter Katherine, who rushed outside to join the search. She called her husband to let him know. Their cleaning helper joined in, combing through the neighborhood, hoping to find Bali.

After almost an hour of searching and calling, it soon became evident that he had escaped from their yard and was no longer in the neighborhood. The wife made the tough decision to call the police department's precinct. Sadly, they could not provide any information about her missing pet, so they suggested speaking to one of their detectives, who often handled such cases.

The husband requested another doctor to cover his shift at the hospital and rushed home. Tatiana, who held a

PhD in Criminal Law, awaited the detective's arrival impatiently. Her husband Manuel wasted no time and used his 'Computer Assistant' installed in their residence to locate and call the best private detective in the area.

"Hello, Mr. LaVell? We are sorry to disturb you on your busy Monday, but we urgently require your assistance locating our dog, Bali."

After listening carefully, detective LaVell added, "No need to apologize or say more. Please, give me your address and personal details. One needs to get used to the unexpected when raising a puppy. Anyway, I'll be there in a few minutes," replied Mr. LaVell. Detective LaVell's confident, smooth tone reassured the couple and filled them with confidence that he would help them find their missing dog. He exuded a sense of authority with each word, instilling trust and confidence in his abilities.

It was disheartening that the police had not prioritized the puppy's disappearance. The assigned detective decided to focus on other pending cases, which frustrated the Hashbun family. Dr. Manuel's decision to involve Detective LaVell was the best idea because he was the only hope for this family to receive the attention this case deserved.

Sure enough, not much time passed before Detective LaVell arrived at the Hashbuns residence as promised. He came with all the documents and forms to allow him to act on their behalf to investigate the disappearance and prompt recovery of that little puppy named Bali. Detective LaVell was a tall man with broad shoulders, a sharp, angular face, and piercing blue eyes that seemed to miss nothing. His tailored suit, fedora, and trench coat exuded a sense of authority and professionalism.

The faint scent of cologne, a mix of musk and sandalwood, lingered around Detective LaVell, adding a sense of moral character to his mysterious aura. Mr. LaVell was considered a pioneer in the modern world of corporate fraud investigations. However, he occasionally took on non-commercial cases, such as the search for Bali. He honestly took this case because Dr. Hashbun's reputation as a renowned doctor and his wife, a distinguished lawyer, may help establish valuable new connections.

Detective LaVell lived on the outskirts of the well-heeled' neighborhood, which was still a high-upper-class community. Unlike most of his close neighbors born into wealth, he had to work hard to build his successful career. It was not luck that set him apart from other professionals. It was his dedication to long hours of fieldwork and top-quality investigations, using the expertise of the best specialists and professionals in the market. He never let the cost of services be an obstacle, nor did he seek to cut expenses to get more significant benefits. His integrity cost him, even so, in the long run, it led him to the top of his profession. Besides, he possessed a natural investigative talent and an ambition that many other skilled investigators lacked.

That afternoon, the topic of Bali dominated the conversation for over an hour and a half. Detective LaVell had to complete some paperwork on his laptop before saying goodbye to Bali's owners. Before concluding his notes, Mr. LaVell asked a trick question. "You say Bali's face color is golden, but corgis are mostly light fawn." The Hashbun couple looked at each other as if suppressing laughter. "Bali's color is so subjective; only when you see him in person will you understand the dilemma," Dr. Manuel added. So, as soon as he concluded the paperwork, he dove right back into the new investigation on his hands. The Hashbuns were fortunate enough that Mr. LaVell had recently completed a highly lucrative job, leaving him time to research this case at leisure.

"We reached him at the right moment," Dr. Manuel thought. It was like they received the answer to their prayers when asking for help in finding Bali. Besides, Dr. Manuel accepted the fee without hesitation and even doubled it for the next six months so that Mr. LaVell could focus solely on finding Bali. Time was paramount, and the Hashbuns and Mr. Lavell knew it. The first 48 hours were crucial when searching for a lost pet.

Mr. LaVell immediately set off to visit the neighbors, starting with the ones on the west side of the house, as the bushes there gave him a hint about Bali's escape. As he approached that corner of the fence, he observed a recent disturbance in the bushes. He didn't dig enough to find the little exit point Bali used. He first knocked on the neighbor's door on the house's west side.

He took his fedora out, showed his face to the security camera, and showed his business card to those at the other end of the camera's lenses. The neighbor took a few minutes to answer him and some more before opening the door. She was not in a good mood to talk because she immediately clarified that she was busy with housework. In the end, she had no problem spending a few minutes with the detective, given that her computer assistant had already verified his credentials—a very reputable one.

When Mr. LaVell asked the neighbor about Bali, "The neighbors' dog?" The old lady responded without remorse, "No, I haven't seen that unruly puppy of my neighbors." Deep down, she knew precisely what Bali did. She enjoyed watching her enemies, those haughty neighbors she despised, suffer a little longer before considering revealing any information.

"Thank you for your cooperation," said Mr. LaVell before leaving, respecting her privacy despite his gut feelings.

He couldn't rid himself of the suspicion that she was aware of something, yet he couldn't compel her to speak. Before going, he turned around, contemplating his surroundings. Mr. John LaVell also noted all the security cameras installed in the house. He walked around the vegetation in the house, which Bali may have used to hide or as an instrument to escape the cameras. "Like he knew what he was doing," the detective thought. "But come on, he's just a little doggy," was his one response.

Mr. LaVell speedily returned to his extravagant mansion, a sense of unease creeping over him as the urgent barks of a distant dog shattered the quiet neighborhood. In a nearby mansion, chaos erupted as alarms blared and lights flashed, signaling the success of a group of skilled thieves who had broken into more than one house.

--- --- ---

Back to our two amigos.

They were the ones who intruded on the houses mentioned before. Now, desperate to escape, they faced a ferocious guard dog and two sleek drones bearing down on them. These advanced machines were linked to the state-of-the-art artificial intelligence security system that fiercely protected that wealthy owner's property. "No trespassers would get away unscathed" was the motto of the security company serving those houses.

The old man's heart raced as he fended off the snarling dog, desperately searching for something to protect himself. His fingers clenched around a sharp piece of tree branch, his knuckles turning white from the pressure. Meanwhile, his partner, the one with the fiery red hair, struggled to unlock the digital service door, their lives hanging in the balance. Each passing second felt like an eternity as they waited for the door to open, fueled by adrenaline and the fear of what might wait for them on the other side. The tension was palpable as they braced themselves for the inevitable confrontation with law enforcement once the door finally opened.

With trembling hands, the young man struggled to push open the stubborn door. It seemed like an hour had passed trying to open the service exit door. When he finally opened it, he discovered that it had been barely six minutes or less. They slipped outside and quickly shut the door behind them. Their hearts raced as the oldest frantically searched for his phone, hoping to get an Uber driver as soon as possible to escape. As he dialed for a driver, doubts crept in—what if the police were already on their trail? Luckily, there was an Uber just two minutes from them.

As they sped away in the Uber, they couldn't shake off the adrenaline coursing through their veins, but underneath it all was a nagging feeling of guilt and uncertainty about what they had just done. The police lights blurred past them as they headed toward their getaway destination—a shopping plaza that seemed worlds away from the tension and danger they had left behind.

As the sunset let its shadows in over the small-town square plaza, our friends quickly stopped at the gas station to freshen up before finding a new hotel. The redhead, known for his appetite, declared to the old man, "I'm starving!" He suggested grabbing snacks at the gas station before finding another car to take them back to a hotel.

However, the old man had other plans. "Or... we could pick up the car first and then swing by Tim Hortons," he insisted.

"No, I need a proper meal. Maybe we can stop at McDonald's," the youngest added.

"You can always grab something at Tim's Drive-Thru if you want," Ben suggested.

After scouring the parking lot for a car to steal, they quickly found a semi-autonomous electric vehicle like the others they had successfully stolen many times. As the oldest was unlocking the doors and getting ready to enter, Bali suddenly appeared in the small open road plaza's parking lot. Without hesitation, he hopped into the car with the two villains when the passenger door opened. Scrambling over the center console, Bali settled into the backseat while the old man questioned his partner about their new passenger.

"What is this? Why is there a dog in our car?" the old man asked incredulously.

"Well, it seems like he wants to join us," his partner smiled with a smile.

"Can't we leave him here? He'll ruin our plan," complained the elder.

But his partner insisted on keeping the little dog, so they drove off toward their next destination—McDonald's for a quick lunch. As soon as they arrived, they treated Bali to water and a hamburger, which he devoured in seconds. Once they had satisfied their hunger, they stopped at Tim Hortons across the street for coffee.

"A triple-triple, for me. Would you like anything?" the graybeard asked his friend as they pulled up to the drive-thru window.

"I'll have an iced tea," responded his partner.

After a long day of scheming and petty crimes, they opted to forgo their usual hotels in the bustling city center and retreated to a dingy motel near the Bullet Train station. The room smelled of stale cigarette smoke and cheap air freshener.

At the moment they were unpacking, the television aired a special news segment about the vanishing of a unique Fijian albino greenish iguana, capturing Bali's attention and instilling in him a newfound fascination for this extraordinary species he had never laid eyes on before.

"Silence, doggy" Ginger shouted in an angry tone without noticing what had made Bali uneasy. So, after settling into the room and exhausted from their misdeeds, the oldest of the two thieves reached for his phone and dialed their boss in New York City—his fingers leaving greasy smears on his phone's screen. The neon lights outside flickered, casting an eerie glow over the shadowy surroundings. Outside, the distant sound of a train rumbling by could be heard, adding to the gritty atmosphere of their hideout.

"Hello, Boss." The old man's voice was strained as he spoke.

"Hey, Ben. How's everything going?" The boss's tone was a little tense. Immediately, he added: "Are you calling from a secure line?"

"Yes, Boss. Everything is alright… I guess." Ben hesitated before continuing. "We did well today. Scored some credit cards, watches, gold chains… and other valuable documents you might be able to sell on the dark web."

"We'll see when you return to the city," the boss replied coolly.

"Ben, I wanted to ask you: Did you go to check the information about the house on 47th Street?" The boss asked.

"Well, …I was busy that afternoon when you asked me to do it. So, no, I haven't checked it yet," Ben responded.

"What were you doing," the boss insisted.

"Um… I do not remember," he riposted.

"Ok, we'll talk about that later," the boss replied.

"Very well, Boss! Now, there's something else," Ben said, his voice faltering.

"What is it?"

"Ginger, he… got himself a puppy. A Corgi."

The boss let out an exasperated sigh. "Why did he have to do that? It's one more complication!"

"I don't know, boss. You'd have to ask him yourself. He's right here next to me."

An unfamiliar voice for the boss spoke up on the line.

"Hello, boss. My name is Renato, but my friends call me Reto."

The boss took a deep breath before addressing him.

"Oh! Yes! Yes… yes. It's okay, Ginger.

So tell me. Why did you have to take in that dog?"

"It wasn't like that, boss. He came to me, and there might be a reward since he comes from a wealthy neighborhood."

The boss fell silent for a moment before responding.

"Fine. We'll look into it when you return to New York City."

"However, I really need to tell you this because dogs are not for everyone. Anyone who has a dog also has a responsibility. They depend completely on us to survive. Can you understand what I am saying?"

"Sure, Boss!" Ginger's voice held a hint of relief.

"Goodbye, Ben. Goodbye, Ginger. See you soon, guys."

The call ended with a click, and Ben and Ginger exchanged wary looks before returning to examine their haul.

Bali Goes Back to The Future

In the buzzing city of Seoul, South Korea, in the year 2042, the renowned scientist from the United States, Dr. Motuo Locus, was giving a riveting lecture on the quantum teleportation of sub-nanoparticles using sympathetic atomic frequencies in the process. The streets outside were alive with neon lights lit twenty-four hours a day and chatters in multiple languages. Still, inside the lecture hall, all eyes were fixed on Dr. Locus as he delved into his research's complexities.

His work had the potential to revolutionize the understanding of time and space, and these possibilities ignited the collective imagination. The potential impacts on world marketing for big industries left him eager to continue his discourse about his groundbreaking work, which could change the course of history as they knew it.

As the final words of his lecture hung in the air, he wasted no time retreating to his quarters. There was no time for pleasantries or small talk (at this time) as he mentally co-ordinated a last-minute plan because of an unexpected incident that captured the attention of scientists worldwide. His mind was consumed with an urgent plan that couldn't wait another second. The urgency of it all fueled his steps as he rushed through the vibrant city streets and finally arrived at his luxury temporary lodging, his heart pounding with the weight of his mission.

After concluding his lecture, his mind wandered to a breaking news story about a dog that had mysteriously appeared out of thin air in a recording studio yesterday evening. The bizarre and unexplainable nature of this event immediately caught his attention. He couldn't avoid wondering if there was more to this phenomenon than scientific explanation - perhaps parallel dimensions or alternate teleporting timelines were at play. This news sparked an intriguing thought in Dr. Locus's mind - "Could this be a case of a time-dislocated transfer or teleportation?" he conjectured. His curiosity piqued, he delved deeper into the concept, his mind racing with new theories and hypotheses, each more compelling than the last.

Dr. Locus knew he needed to examine that dog, that crucial piece of evidence, as soon as possible, at any cost. The dog, he realized, could hold the key to unlocking the mysteries of corporeal regrouping or molecular reconstruction in the time of displacement of sub-nanoparticles. With determination burning in his veins, he decided, as a first step, to call the local police to claim ownership of the puppy.

So, he contacted his headquarters in the USA and arranged for an interpreter to assist him in acquiring vital information about the dog's whereabouts. Next, he made a three-way telephone call to the Seoul Police Department with an interpreter at the other end of the phone call. He carefully explained to the officers in Seoul that the puppy had escaped and he was desperately searching for him.

As mysterious as it may seem, the extravagant and luxurious place where Dr. Locus was staying was not too far from the filming studio where Bali appeared. One of many around the city that the company owns for filming its productions. Therefore, his story about going for a walk with his puppy and the pup getting away was totally credible, and the police were willing to investigate it.

There were no worries about the manifesto at the airport as he traveled on his private electric supersonic jet and only declared, "traveling with personal belongings." That minimalist detail in the description allowed him to include many things among his personal belongings, including a puppy. In addition, he traveled with so many packages that it would be impossible to see in the airport videos if one of them actually contained the claimed dog.

As soon as those calls were finalized, he dialed his talented special agent, 'Lila.' With a clear and concise tone through a secured line, Dr. Motuo instructed her to obtain fraudulent documents showing the ownership of a Corgi with identical descriptions to the one that debuted in the popular soap opera 'Kisses and Tears,' a day ago. After providing her with all the necessary information, he firmly stated, "I need those documents here in Seoul within three days. Get everything ready and start packing —I need them brought to me immediately."

The day after Bali's unexpected appearance in the filming studio, the news spread worldwide through formal and informal news media. The soap opera producers were at a loss at what to do with him. However, they decided to keep him confined to an enclosed space within iron bars. They hoped to find his owners and potentially offer Bali a role in their soap opera for the ten-season. So, to keep him safe, the manager ordered one of the janitors to look after Bali.

On that daybreak, as the morning sun streamed into the studio, its rays illuminated the dusty air, and the janitor ventured out searching for Bali. To his surprise, he discovered the playful dog roaming freely amidst the props and equipment. Sensing it was time for the dog's bathroom break, the janitor led Bali outside into the spacious fenced yard at the back of the studio property. As they strolled, he suddenly heard a faint yet distinct voice whispering in his ear: "*Time to eat.*" Confused but trusting his instincts, he quickly realized that Bali must be hungry and thirsty.

As the janitor walked Bali around the studio, he noticed how well-behaved and friendly the dog was. He wondered how someone could abandon or neglect the watch for even a second of such a lovable animal. Suddenly, he remembered the producers' decision to keep Bali in an enclosed space and the idea of offering him a role in their soap opera. The janitor couldn't avoid feeling a pang of sadness for the dog's uncertain future. As they reached the studio's cafeteria, Bali eagerly wagged his tail and barked happily at the janitor.

He instinctively knew that this was the place to get food. Perhaps the smells of food or the sight of people sitting and eating. Still, he heard again that voice telling him: "*Time to eat.*" The janitor smiled and patted Bali's head, grateful for the opportunity to care for him. As they sat down to eat, the janitor couldn't avoid thinking Bali would make a perfect addition to his family. With a bit of persuasion, he managed to get Bali some pieces of turkey and chicken for breakfast.

As the day went on, the janitor continued to care for Bali, taking him for walks, feeding him with some small pieces of peanut butter treats, and even teaching him a few new tricks. He couldn't imagine the dog being again confined to a space behind bars. Then, the janitor considered adopting him because Bali's owners may never be found -he thought. As he watched Bali playfully chasing after a ball, the janitor couldn't stop feeling that this was the beginning of a beautiful friendship.

Unfortunately for the janitor, he had forgotten a couple of things. The first was the presence of cameras all around the studio. The second was the increased intrigue and interest created by the producers over Bali's acting abilities. They were captivated by the famous event of Bali's appearance at the live filming of the soap opera the day before. Therefore, at the end of the day, when a security agent saw the janitor trying to leave the studio with the puppy, he was immediately arrested by the security agent in service that night at the studio. The local police soon arrived to apprehend the janitor despite his good intentions.

The company's interests were above all other considerations. Unfortunately for Bali, he had to return to his temporary confinement that night again. Because of Bali's mood, one could say that he surprisingly missed the janitor who had so quickly gained his trust. He was not an animal that easily trusted strangers, but he had an instinct or intuition to be able to interpret the intentions of those people of good character.

On the second day after Bali debuted on the popular soap opera 'Kisses and Tears,' the upper management sprang into action. They assigned three private detectives as Bali's companions to accompany him in 8-hour shifts, ensuring he had round-the-clock supervision. And as if that wasn't enough, the leading producer demanded an immediate complete medical examination for their newest star. Thanks to advanced technology, the lab's test and X-ray results returned early that afternoon, revealing a shocking discovery: a small microchip was attached to Bali's brain.

The vet's eyes glinted ominously; he probably intuited that a government secret was implanted within the dog's brain. "Still, will this microchip alter the very thoughts of the doggy?" Other questions raced through the vet's mind—"Who put it there? What does it do? Is it related to his sudden rise to fame?" The atmosphere around Bali was suddenly charged with mystery and intrigue as one of the assistants commented on the findings with the leading producer. All these findings added a new layer of complexity to his already captivating presence on screen.

Scientifically speaking, the microchip got implanted in Bali's brain for two reasons. First, the technology was not advanced enough to teleport multiple objects simultaneously. Second, when the dematerialized sub-nanoparticles were reintegrated through a molecular reconstruction, the computer assumed this microchip was part of his brain. It could have been something random or by assimilation due to the microchip functions. Nonetheless, now that the algorithms of the complex electronic brains have mapped it in that area, it will remain there in his next teleportation.

Furthermore, the veterinarian, a seasoned expert in his field, was left speechless by Bali's incredible abilities. The dog's sleek black coat shimmered under the bright lights of the vet's private practice office. Bali's muscles rippled with unexpected movements as he reacted to every stimulus inflicted. His nose, a powerful tool that could detect even the faintest scents, twitched with excitement as he took an interest in all the aromas with which he was tested that day. His ears, alert and perked like finely tuned antennas, could pick up on the slightest rustle or whisper of sound. Moreover, his eyes, one deep sediment of amber and the other blue like an ocean, worked as well-adjusted binoculars. Bali seemed to hold immense intelligence and was sharp and focused as he scanned the room, looking at all the visual cues intentionally implanted in that room, specifically for the test.

As the veterinarian put Bali through various tests and challenges, the dog's responses were not only good; they were simply astounding. He seemed to understand and execute several commands effortlessly, and his success rate reached an impeccable one hundred percent of perfection. It was clear that Bali was not an ordinary canine - he was a truly exceptional being capable of understanding the 200 commands tested on that day. This revelation left everyone close to him astonished at Bali's capabilities.

The minds of those in close contact or with access to his data were whirring with questions and amazement at the sheer brilliance of this remarkable animal. The mystery of Bali's extraordinary abilities hung in the air, leaving everyone intrigued and captivated. "How could a dog possess such extraordinary abilities?" questioned the veterinarian. "What other surprises may lay behind those intelligent eyes?" he was intrigued.

On the third day after his appearance on the hit soap opera "Kisses and Tears," the distinguished and renowned veterinarian returned to the bustling studio with his trusty assistant to pick up Bali for another round of tests. The leading producer in charge raised a skeptical eyebrow as she asked, "More tests? How is this possible?" but the vet remained steadfast and responded, "The truth is, this puppy has incredible abilities, and I want to document all of them." A couple of minutes later, one of the three dog's companions finally spoke up after silently observing the interaction between the leading producer and the veterinarian from the corner of the room.

"I can vouch for what the vet said. Last night, I locked him in his confinement space, and he managed to escape," he added. "Was the security bolt slid all the way in?" asked the leading producer. "Sure, it was. However, the next morning, I found him trolling outside, wandering around the garden," the dog's companion said. He stopped his discourse for a second, looking at the room's ceiling with his right hand over his mouth.

He placed the tip of his right thumb on his chin with his index finger touching his upper lip and added: "...And during mealtimes, he speaks to me, telling me 'It's time to eat." The room fell into shocked silence as the dog's companion continued. "But he doesn't actually make any sounds - it's like he communicates with me telepathically or somehow without talking." The leading producer's eyes widened in amazement as she exclaimed, "Well, does this puppy... have powers?" This revelation left the audience with a sense of surprise and intrigue.

The vet looked everyone around in the eyes. At the same time, his gaze was fixed on Bali. The puppy was sitting innocently by the door of his room, wagging his tail in excitement. "I'm not sure; it seems like he has some enhancements," he admitted, scratching his head in bewilderment. "I've never seen anything like this before." Bali's companion chimed in again, a mix of concern and awe in his voice, "And there's something else. Sometimes, I found objects on the floor that the night before were secured on the shelves above him."

The room was filled with a sense of wonder and curiosity as they all turned to look at Bali, who tilted his head quizzically. Finally, the leading producer broke the silence, her big green eyes sparkling with intrigue. "These findings may not mean anything," she declared with a hint of excitement in her voice. "We need to learn more about this puppy and his extraordinary abilities. Imagine the possibilities!" The vet and Bali's companion exchanged a knowing glance.

Notwithstanding, after twenty-two minutes and fifteen seconds of a conversation full of speculations, common sense suddenly came to the producer's head. She looked intensely into the horizon and thought clearly about this situation. "Wait a minute, you guys are jumping to conclusions too quickly." She stopped talking and looked everyone around straight in the eyes. "Why haven't any security officers commented or said anything? Could it be that they saw nothing?" Everyone was perplexed by the clarity of thought the leading producer displayed.

She continued with her exposé: "Besides, there are so many factors to consider or reasons why the items could have fallen to the floor or the gate got open: a rat, the wind through an open window, a raccoon, another animal, or even a careless employee who didn't check the sliding bolt." She paused for a second to gather her last thoughts. "The fact is, there are no cameras in this little warehouse we've placed Bali in. I will ask management to order CCTV cameras so everything is documented."

The vet immediately responded, "What about my test results?" She immediately added: "Well, a dog with a good sense of smell, hearing, and vision doesn't make him a super-hero. Neither does his ability to respond to over 200 commands. In fact, the dogs used by the police and the military already have that ability." She moved closer to the vet and said, "But it's okay. Take him and complete whatever tests you deem necessary to clear this up. Please, don't say a word of this to anyone until we have conclusive evidence." Just like that, she ended the conversation and left.

The vet took Bali for another day of medical tests. Bali's physical examinations continued all day long. Without a doubt, he can smell much better than any other dog he was compared to. He can also hear commands from much greater distances than any other animal. What's even more intriguing is that he can differentiate between over 1,000 words without any confusion, suggesting that he has the potential to acquire even more knowledge.

On the fourth day, the producers kept a secret from the rest of the crew: The police showed up at the station's door to inform them that the dog's possible owner was reclaiming him. Nonetheless, the police detective assigned to the case has not yet had time to review all the documents. For all that, the leading producer was instructed to keep Bali inside the instal-lation, protected and under constant surveillance. So, not to keep him locked up, she decided to let Bali train for the soap opera's filming. In case the owner decided to let him perform in the soap opera. His training involved responding to the coach's commands, following the script, and understanding the actions required for his role.

Bali responded to the coach's commands to interact with the other actors without a problem. It would seem that Bali knew the script. However, the coach who communicated the commands to him was the one who read the instructions from the script. Or did Bali really know the script? Bali's flawless performance during the rehearsal was a sight to behold. His impeccable behavior and splendid acting skills left everyone in the crew in awe. Not a single repetition was needed because of any mistake from Bali, further cementing his status as a remarkable dog.

On the fifth day, A police officer came to the site with some documents that required the immediate attention of the television station's legal department. Still, a few errors their Lawyer found will delay any immediate action regarding Bali. First, not all documents were officially translated into the South Korean language. Second, some seals from local government offices were missing. The third and most crucial erratum was that the town taxes for the homologation of foreign documents from the United States had not been paid.

So, given that the legal department has had to intervene, Bali couldn't leave the studio under any circumstances from now on. Any action involving the little dog with small legs must be consulted with the legal department first. The studio couldn't risk any lawsuit regarding Bali from such a powerful American firm as Locus Enterprise LLC. So, Bali was under constant surveillance but well-fed, and he had tons of toys and bones to play with, which he enjoyed all day long. Furthermore, regardless of any claims or complaints from any mid-management officials, the senior executives used their authoritarian prerogative when they issued these ordinances governing Bali's permanency on the company's property. So, they had decided to preserve Bali in the best possible conditions until his legal ownership could be clarified.

On the sixth day, Lila arrived at the film company's offices with a South Korean police officer, claiming Bali. She completed all the necessary paperwork in one day. Incredibly, Lila obtained all the required paperwork and permits, satisfying all the demands from the South Korean government to bring or return Bali to the United States. Her sudden appearance raised more questions about Bali's inexplicable arrival at the studio and the reasons for her hasty demand. All these added a new layer of mystery to Bali's story. Yet, armed with indisputable evidence, Lila had complete control over the dog's ownership and couldn't be stopped from taking him.

The producers were desperate and offered Lila a considerable sum of money to persuade her boss, Dr. Locus, to let Bali continue acting in the soap opera. However, Lila had strict orders from Dr. Motuo Locus, the renowned American scientist and entrepreneur, to retrieve Bali and bring him back to the United States at once. He couldn't personally take care of this action due to his previous commitments back in the USA. And there was no way to persuade Lila, not even with the once-in-a-lifetime opportunity of a five million contract for five years, to let Bali perform.

Lila was pressured to fulfill her mission, and there was not enough money to prevent her from bringing Bali to Dr. Motuo. Perhaps an absurd amount of money, like a billion dollars, might pique her interest. After all, her loyalty was only focused on money. Fortunately, Dr. Locus knew how to compensate for her services, not only with enough money but also with constant replenishment.

– – –

Bali is now in Toronto in 2042

As the seventh day dawned, Bali finally arrived at the Locus Enterprise's experimental plant in Toronto, where Dr. Locus awaited him. The brand-new building was a three-floor structure of gleaming metal and glass, bristling with state-of-the-art technology. Among its many wonders were a couple of experimental machines designed to transfer or teleport disintegrated sub-nanoparticles to a predetermined coordinate to reintegrate the molecular matter of the objects there. Although it was in its early stages to be compared against the one developed by Dr. Wojcik in 2051, it also had structural errors. If only these two brilliant minds had been working together, there is no doubt that their project would be running at total capacity in the year 2042.

Yet, the insurmountable barriers of pride and misunderstanding distanced the two geniuses of quantum mechanics. This rift would not only delay progress in this science field for a decade but also cast a shadow over their collaborations' potential. So, in his desperation for success, Dr. Locus often searched for the royal road, looking to shorten the time, and ended in some failed detours. His results never proved to be what he had hoped for. Several years later, his colleague would produce the quantum transfer of dispersed matter in sub-nanoparticles to be reintegrated again in its entirety in a dislocated coordinate. Unbeknownst to anyone, Bali was the first successful case of teleportation or dematerialization in something less than sub-nanoparticles to be re-materialized elsewhere.

Upon his arrival to Canada from the USA, as Bali stepped inside the central lab of Locus Enterprise LLC, he marveled at the sight of scientists scurrying about. The glow of computer screens illuminated their faces, and the hum of machinery filled the air. This was indeed a place where innovation thrived, and anything seemed possible. It also seemed familiar to Bali, in a way, as he was present in its collapse in 2050. On the day of his arrival, Dr. Motuo was so busy coordinating efforts to open his second lab in Toronto that he didn't have time to spend with the pup. Bali, meanwhile, was so disoriented that he just watched everything surrounding him with very little interaction. Besides, he was still unaware of his exceptional abilities.

Undoubtedly, Dr. Locus's lab stood as a shining beacon of technological advancement in 2042. The sleek, modern design and state-of-the-art equipment made it the envy of researchers across the globe. However, little did Dr. Locus know that his colleague Dr. Wojcik would surpass him with a more advanced, even though less luxurious, laboratory in only a little less than a decade. For now, Dr. Motuo was making groundbreaking progress with his teleportation research, pushing the boundaries of scientific discovery. Unfortunately, a few years later, he would make a costly mistake due to insufficient data verification, causing him to shift his focus to a different approach, and this allowed his rival to get ahead of him and make significant strides in their sub-nanoparticle quantum teleportation machine's project.

By a twist of fate, something surprising happened when Dr. Locus's technology developed in 2042 was combined with the microchip from 2051 that had been integrated into Bali's brain anatomy. Without knowing it, Dr. Locus accidentally teleported Bali back to 2051, matching the closest dimension manipulated by Bali's mind. He teleported him back to the dimension closest to his thoughts after recollecting a photo of Dr. Motuo with Dr. Wojcik in the latter's house hallway.

Bali remembered those faces in a portrait at the entrance to another lab in Buffalo, New York, passing through the living room to the laboratory office on Dr. David Wojcik's house. Bali only visited once and disappeared, but with the enhancement in his brain, he finds it easy to recall many past events. That thought became a dimensional window. So, he was transferred to the Wojcik residence hallway near the living room, where engineer Jennifer Williams liked to sit and watch soap operas.

— — —

Bali is now in Toronto in 2051

Bali was accidentally teleported into the future due to the microchip embedded in his brain. This artificial intelligence computing device was ten years more advanced than all the computer systems Dr. Locus Enterprise LLC was using then. Thus, its ability to self-generate intelligence gave it control over the system to set up all the sequences necessary for Bali's teleportation. Unfortunately, Dr. Locus will not be able to replicate it because the microchip did not need to store any information to complete its maneuvers. There is a record, though, of the activity, something incomprehensible to the computer science professionals in the year 2042, yet not totally baffling to the intellectual capacity of Dr. Motuo Locus.

Dr. Locus was now absorbed in his meditation about what had happened, as he couldn't understand after three months in oblivion. The truth is that Bali couldn't forget the memories of the future (back at home in 2051). So, he proved useless to Dr. Motuo due to his lack of cooperation.

Bali didn't perform well in the investigations conducted by the scientists under Dr. Locus. However, before returning to the Future, Bali himself proved that he was critical to better understanding the quantum teleportation of sub-nanoparticles and its later molecular reconstruction. This is thanks to the microchip now integrated into his brain. Yet, in 2042, it was too late for Dr. Locus to understand his failure because he didn't find a way to motivate the little canine that hid an essential piece of advanced technology in his brain.

Let's review what happened that afternoon when Dr. Locus was experimenting with the dematerialization and reintegration of quantum sub-nanoparticles in the little platforms of his extraordinary lab. He didn't notice that Bali was walking around and observing; one might say that he was analyzing the whole operation. Well, it was not him, but his brain interconnecting with the computers. Then he stopped walking and sat down on one of the small improvised teleporter's platforms from where he disappeared.

PuuuuuuuumN! A sudden, jarring, and loud sound echoed across the room. It sounded like a truck tire blowing out on the highway. And just like that, Bali disappeared from the room without a trace. Only the lab cameras captured the teleportation since everything happened in fractions of a second. Dr. Locus would later watch this video millions of times, wondering where his research on the fascinating short-legged canine went wrong.

Once again, Bali was teleported by accident. Yes, this was his second time in the sequence of events of his life, and the first will later be revealed. This time, he went back to the Future in 2051. Bali was transferred to the dimension closest to his thoughts in the Wojcik's hallway in his house located in Buffalo, New York. He arrived at the Wojcik house and immediately moved to the living room, where Jennifer was watching a popular South Korean soap opera rerun. As per Jennifer, there was not enough time in the day to immerse oneself in the sorrows and anguish imagined by others about realities probably experienced by millions of spectators in their real lives. That was ninety days before the other Bali from the Future was teleported or transferred to the Past in 2042.

– – –

Back to Dr. Wojcik's office lab in 2051.

In 2051, upon discovering the intrusion of a doggy in his house, Doctor Wojcik, without much thought, released a local alert in the formal and informal media to locate the owners. Lila was on it; she had already been notified well in advance. In fact, she met Bali in 2042, even though she never knew what happened to him after she delivered him to Dr. Locus.

Although he was aware that Lila knew of the existence of Bali, he emphasized to her that she should be alert for the sudden appearance of a dog in the near future. He had his hunch and was always expecting the appearance of Bali somewhere on the planet any day after he disappeared a little over eight years ago. Dr. Locus has been searching in the media for all those years himself.

Now, Lila, in 2051, with her worldwide spy networks, intercepted the message and sent a couple of collaborators pretending to be a couple to pick up Bali with fraudulent papers. That was the Bali that the thief Ben saw passing in front of him on his way out of the Bullet Train parking lot the day he and Ginger had arrived in Toronto. Dr. Motuo instructed Lila to take Bali to an experimental station in Quebec, and she was en route there in an electric flying limousine when Ben saw the Bali from 2042 back to the Future three months after his first teleportation.

The Story of Motuo and David

Mr. Locus met Mr. Wojcik in the third session of their PhD program in Quantum Mechanics. They took the "Materials Science" class at the School of Quantum Mechanics in the Faculty of Engineering at the University at Buffalo. This program began gaining popularity and had only been implemented in Buffalo, New York, about seven years earlier. Nestled within the prestigious SUNY University at Buffalo's Engineering Department, the program was a shining gem of innovation and opportunity.

With its state-of-the-art technology and cutting-edge courses, the "Materials Science" class quickly became the talk of the campus. Students were eager to enroll in its dynamic classes and work alongside renowned professors, pushing the boundaries of traditional engineering. Its success, spreading beyond the university walls, had garnered attention from industry leaders and potential employers, solidifying its reputation as one of the most promising programs in the nation.

Motuo and David emerged from the classroom, their voices excitedly as they eagerly discussed the topics of their third session. The crowded hallway was a blur of students rushing to get to their next class, yet the two friends were completely engrossed in their conversation. They moved through the chaos with ease, sidestepping and dodging the sea of bodies with practiced precision. As they made their way toward their next destination, their energy seemed to pulse and surge like a live wire, fueled by the thrill of their upcoming project. With each step, they could feel their anticipation growing, like electricity coursing through their veins. Like brave explorers setting out on an expedition into uncharted territory. They were eager to uncover new discoveries and knowledge together, united by a shared sense of adventure and curiosity.

They immediately noticed each other's mutual passion for the subject. They engaged in a lively conversation about the day's lesson, sharing ideas and debating different technical approaches with palpable excitement in their voices. At that moment, it seemed they were the only two on campus. So engrossed they were in their intellectual exchange concerning splitting matter into sub-nanoparticles. The passion for science shone in their eyes as they quarreled, each defending his point of view with solid arguments and detailed examples. Mr. David and Mr. Motuo continued their lively discussion as they walked through the crowded halls of the University at Buffalo.

Their friendship was unbreakable, but their intellectual rivalry was a constant, a testament to their passion for knowledge. Both were erudite in their understanding of 'quantum physics,' and their intellectual prowess was undeniably superior to the rest of the class. Some would even argue that they grasped certain subjects better than their professors. However, one day, the Quantum Physics III professor presented a complex problem in the classroom, sparking a wave of wonderment and admiration among the students for their unparalleled knowledge.

Unlike David, Motuo was incredibly articulate, giving him a significant advantage in any public debate. But pride is a challenging thing to appease. Therefore, David also expressed his opinion on the problem at hand. The debate intensified, and as they delved deeper into the logic of the subject, the fear of making a mistake that would tarnish their reputation as intelligent students began to paralyze some of their classmates. Those refrained from expressing their opinions, withdrawing from the discussion one by one until only Motuo and David remained.

David asked permission to demonstrate his arguments at the height of his discussion. He went to the front to write his equations on the holographic screen pad. Luckily, the course time for this session lasted three hours, and the professor did not want to interrupt the debate since it seemed he was also learning something from his students. David very quickly wrote his formulas using the "digital typing pad" from where they were reflected on the holographic screens in the classroom. He had created about four screens of formulas when suddenly, another of the students stopped him to make a correction. This was Miguel Reyes, a brilliant student from Santo Domingo, Dominican Republic, with a promising future.

Miguel asked David to go back about seven steps in his equations where, as a good physics expert, he pointed out an error in the original equation from which David had developed other calculations on which he based his leading theory. Motuo, who was watching all the action from his seat, wasted no time corroborating any revision because he had also silently developed his own formulas separately.

However, when Motuo heard Miguel's words, they made him connect David's mistake with what had already been on his notes. This was the moment he had been waiting to speak, and without further ado, he stood up from his seat and projected his equations with the corrections detected by Miguel. As Motuo was an expert in rhetoric, the words flowed from his mouth like a cascade of knowledge, falling off the Quantum Physics basin cliff to the audience attending the class that day. His correction not only improved David's theory but also enriched the understanding of the entire class.

Motuo emerged victorious from the discussion, his head held high, and his pride rose in the sky. David even had to admit his mistake and bear witness to Motuo's calculations. In reality, David was more interested in knowledge itself than in competition. However, that day, all the other forty-seven students in the class received one of the best lectures of their lives, shaping their understanding of physics for the rest of their professional lives. Four hours had passed since the beginning of the discussion. Still, no one noticed it until the professor had to ask them to leave the classroom since another professor was waiting for the class to end. Curiously, the other professor did not claim the classroom either because, from the moment he entered, he also immersed himself in Motuo's exposition and was perplexed by the clarity with which he expressed such complicated theories of physics.

So, at the end of the session, the two professors came to congratulate Motuo and talked with him for about twenty-seven minutes after the lecture ended. Even the students from the other session who were entering and beginning to read the formulas and notes were so intrigued that they asked Motuo to explain how he had arrived at his theoretical conclusions. The other professor had no problem because he wanted to hear the whole explanation. So, Motuo spent another two hours uninterrupted, and his audience applauded him at the end of the session. David had already left without having learned of this event. Although David did not hold any resentment against Motuo, he knew this was a more theoretical than an empirical matter.

From that moment on, David had no peace in his thirst to prove his theory and, little by little, every day, at the end of the day and before going to bed, he tried to find a way to prove in practice the concepts discussed in the lecture that day. This unwavering determination was responsible for him eventually discovering the correct equations as testimony to his relentless search for truth. His continuous work and the verification of documented data were what led him to overcome Motuo's rhetoric. But many more years would pass before he can prove himself in practice.

In any case, the two of them were still unbreakable friends at that time, and this event did not change anything in the relationship since, for David, there was no winner or loser. He had also gained knowledge that would have taken him years to discover on his own. Because of this, the two friends continued their everyday lives because even Motuo's super-ego had already become part of his personality before David met him.

On another occasion, Mr. David and Mr. Motuo intensified their discussion of splitting matter into sub-nanoparticles. Their voices echoed through the hallway, attracting curious glances from other students. As they discussed the possible applications of teleporting matter, their minds sparkled with creativity and determination. David firmly held his position with precise focus and clarity in every argument.

At the same time, Motuo, with his infectious enthusiasm and practical experience, challenged each point with innovative examples. Their discussions were not limited to topics of their assigned classes. They shared a world of ideas after every session once a week and then shifted the conversations to cafeterias, restaurants, and dinners. They even started inviting their respective dates or partners. Their minds overflowed with creative inspiration as they enjoyed meals filled with laughter and lively discussion. The aroma of delicious food wafted around them. The chatter of other diners provided a pleasant background noise, but their diverse and curious minds indeed filled the space.

The bond between these two friends grew stronger. They discussed new concepts and bounced ideas off each other, savoring every moment of their time together. Their camaraderie was palpable, creating an atmosphere of warmth and companionship at every encounter. After each delicious meal came the nights of intense reading and hard work on assignments given by their demanding professors. Also, it is worth noting that they spent long hours in the university library, with only occasional interruptions from the gentle rustling of pages and the constant clock ticking.

One night of study was at David's cozy home, surrounded by shelves full of old books, and another was in Motuo's opulent residence, overlooking the moonlit city. Each place had its charm and unique atmosphere, making it perfect for concentrating and achieving academic goals. Luckily, Motuo's family was wealthy, and they financed his studies. David worked a part-time job, and his wife made significant contributions, hoping and trusting that her efforts would be rewarded one day.

At the end of their third semester, it was time to decide on the dissertation topic. So, David and Motuo agreed that combining their experiences in developing a project they could share would be best. After several hours of discussion on this topic, they decided to do a dissertation on the transfer or teleportation of sub-nanoparticles. To interest Motuo, David comments: "The sub-nanoparticle's movement depends on the interplay between the in-plane force and driving force. In contrast, the subsequent transport is determined by the blocks' slip velocity and the damping force. Now the problem is how to use the sympathetic atomic frequencies to reintegrate matters once 'literally' disintegrated?"

Motuo analyzed David's comment and answered: "How can we achieve the quantum transfer of sub-nanoparticles of various sizes without getting distorted by the driving force?" David thought for a few seconds and then answered: "It has been demonstrated in physics that a pre-tensioned graphene substrate improves sub-nanoparticle transportation in their liquid state.

Besides, this new transport mechanism will enable the design of a novel nano sieve that can spontaneously screen and classify sub-nanoparticles of different sizes to a 'nanoscopic' scale. This is essential for the molecular reconstruction of the matter." "Uhmmmm! Interesting" was Motuo's last reaction. For good reasons, after that conversation, he felt that David's knowledge on this topic surpassed his own and felt, for the first time, a sense of awkwardness in their relationship.

On a later day, as David engaged in lively conversation with his university classmates, he was utterly oblivious to Motuo lurking a few steps behind him. Little did he know, Motuo was, by accident, strategically positioned behind another student, eavesdropping on his every word. During the chat, David mentioned a past experience with a close friend, and Motuo's ears perked up. But instead of joining in the conversation, his face contorted with confusion and awkwardness as he listened to David's words.

The anecdote that seemed innocent to David struck a nerve with Motuo—it had happened four years ago during his undergraduate days. Motuo probably thought he was talking about him in a figurative sense. His grip tightened on a glass bottle as he struggled to hold back his emotions, silently seething at David's obliviousness to the impact of his words. From that moment on, Motuo could never see his friendship with David in the same light again.

Motuo thought about joining David's conversation to clarify what he had thought he understood. Still, he preferred to walk away silently from the group under the pretext of going to the bathroom. Obviously, he misinterpreted the conversation, and from that moment on, there was no longer the same spark in his friendship with David.

A feeling of discomfort and displeasure took hold of Motuo, making him feel distant and uncomfortable in the relationship from that moment on. First, a little envy and now a slight misgiving were enough to put some distance between them. Motuo, out of pride, would never admit these feelings. Somehow, these events changed the perception of the relationship between the two amigos. David didn't understand what was happening with Motuo and avoided confronting him, leading to their relationship deteriorating into a void of hypocrisy.

Following the misunderstanding incident, Mr. Motuo's demeanor underwent a drastic transformation. His attitude, once friendly and agreeable, had now changed to a volatile combination of vengeance and competition. Despite his outward appearance remaining unchanged, there is a palpable tension whenever they are in the same room. Despite this animosity, they managed to complete their post-doctoral project together.

They even collaborated on other research, including nanotechnology theory. Much of those studies earned them the highest accolades and academic recognition. Surprisingly, their rivalry did not hinder their individual successes. They have excelled in different studies. Anyhow, unknown to David, Motuo was always scheming for ways to undermine him. It was like Motuo wanted to push him out of their shared field of expertise.

After years of studies, Dr. Motuo finally decided to use his knowledge to open his own company, borrowing from his family's wealth. However, he soon realized that David, his former colleague and friend, was crucial to his enterprise. The success of his company's project may depend on David's knowledge, but he was not invited to join the venture.

Dr. Motuo soon came to terms with the fact that his past projects were only successful with David's contributions. Later, their rivalry became public as they competed for the same projects. They both wanted to create an invaluable sub-nanotechnology to transfer or teleport disintegrated matter. Then, reconstruct their molecular structures in a specific coordinate. Motuo was determined to obtain the necessary information from David at any cost. Desperate, he enlisted the help of a cunning spy named Marsha Ponzi, widely recognized as 'Lila.'

Marsha was born in a household where success was the only measure of worth. Her father, an accountant, and her mother, a third-grade teacher at a Catholic school, instilled in her the importance of hard work and financial stability. However, Marsha could not stop envying her cousins, who inherited a large sum of money from their uncle, who owned a popular pizzeria.

Not only that, but his deceased uncle had also left behind a sizeable life insurance policy worth two million, two hundred seventy thousand, and fifty-five dollars. While her two cousins lived lavish lifestyles and indulged in expensive luxuries, Marsha's parents worked hard to have a middle-class lifestyle. This envy eventually turned into bitter resentment toward her cousins, as she felt she could never compete with their wealth and their subsequent business success.

Then, Marsha stumbled upon a way to make easy money—uncovering secrets among her cousins' wealthy friends and charging for her silence. After obtaining a reward from a client's secret, she buried it (as the best she could), wiping all accessible evidences from the social media websites. With this practice, her bank account grew fatter than those of other professionals in this kind of business, and her thirst for material possessions intensified. She soon gained fame for her investigative skills, and lucky enough; she met a private investigator who took her under his wing and taught her everything she needed to know to become one herself.

Consumed by greed, there was no room for remorse as she destroyed lives and reputations to pursue personal gain, whether social status or financial wealth. The allure of wealth and power has tainted her once pure outlook on success and happiness. At only twenty-five years old, materialism has entirely consumed her, and she has lost sight of what truly matters in life. Family, relationships, hobbies, respect for others, and spiritual beliefs lost all values and didn't mean anything anymore to her.

In a short time, Marsha skillfully integrated herself into David's world as Dr. Motuo requested and soon became intrigued by his passion and dedication to his work. The office lab in the back room of David's residence was a marvel of modern technology, filled with humming machinery and holographic screens displaying complex holographic equations. As she observed in awe, there was machinery connected by very high voltage electrical wires with internal capsules floating by magnetic gravity. All components together showcase David's intense concentration and devotion to experimentation. Every corner of the room reflected his passion for pushing boundaries in scientific discovery.

During his postdoctoral studies, Motuo quickly realized that David held a wealth of knowledge beyond what he had previously thought. Thereupon, he devoted all his attention to understanding and learning everything he could about David's projects. However, as much as he scoured through

David's publications, there were underlying concepts he couldn't grasp directly. That was the reason why Dr. Motuo hired the detective named Marsha Ponzi to act as his spy and gain access to David's discoveries. The idea was to claim such knowledge as his own later on.

Marsha was thirty years younger than Dr. Motuo when she met him, and her intelligence and cunning nature matched her beauty. She didn't hesitate to cross legal boundaries if it meant a substantial financial gain.

It was tricky for Marsha to establish a connection with David at the beginning. Yet, she disguised herself as a saleswoman of technological products secretly negotiated by Dr. Motuo. Only in this way did she gradually gain his trust. Through this strategy, she was able to infiltrate the laboratory and study its security systems until she understood them well enough to plant hidden cameras when nobody was watching.

The situation was almost laughably ironic. Despite the exorbitant amount of money and resources poured into obtaining state-of-the-art spy equipment, it proved utterly useless for Dr. Motuo Locus' ambitions. The sleek gadgets, smuggled in by the cunning Marsha Ponzi, were rendered completely irrelevant by the overpowering interference of David's artifacts. Every attempt at deciphering even the simplest sounds or images was met with frustration and failure, only adding to Dr. Motuo's mounting tension and desperation.

Nonetheless, Dr. Motuo Locus wasn't one to give up easily. Frustration fueled his determination, and he was not about to let some artifacts stand in the way of his grand plans.

With a steely glint in his eyes, he called upon his team of top-notch scientists to come up with a solution. As they huddled together in the dimly lit underground lair, ideas bounced back and forth like charged particles in a reactor.

One of the younger scientists, a brilliant mind named Li Wei, suddenly perked up with an idea. "What if we try to create a frequency disruptor? Something that can counteract the interference from those artifacts?" he suggested, his eyes bright with excitement. Dr. Motuo Locus studied Li Wei for a moment before nodding approvingly. "Yes, yes, that just might work," he murmured, a flicker of hope igniting in his heart. With renewed energy, the team set to work in the strategy on how to steal Dr. David secrets.

"Marsha, get on the preparation of the dimensional disruptor immediately! If we can't spy on them conventionally, we'll just have to bring them to us," Dr. Motuo declared, his voice filled with newfound confidence. Marsha's eyes widened in surprise at the audacity of the plan, but she knew better than to question Dr. Motuo's authority. Nodding quickly, she set to work gathering from the scientist the list of the necessary components for the dimensional disruptor.

A week had passed since the machine was first activated, its low thrum echoing through the underground chamber. Each day, Dr. Motuo's grin grew larger as he eagerly awaited his chance to turn Dr. David's luck around and reclaim his wounded pride. As the hum grew louder and more intense, Dr. Motuo's eyes gleamed with a maniacal determination to succeed at any cost. This was his moment of redemption, and he would stop at nothing to achieve it.

Yet, the technology to block the radio frequencies was not yet there due to the high magnetics fields with which was Dr. David playing with. Also, the Channel overcrowding also seems to be impossible to remedy. This very common sources of interference were overlapping wireless networks from nearby devices in the local area, such as neighboring businesses or public hotspots.

Despite Dr. Motuo's persistent investment in sophisticated spy equipment, the waves generated by high voltages of magnetism seemed determined to hinder any progress. It was a silent war, waged between competing scientists with their own agendas. As Dr. Motuo tirelessly improved his blocking capacity, Dr. David labored to perfect the magnetic fields within the teleportation capsule, striving to eliminate any friction that could impede its exponential rotations.

Dr. David's ultimate goal was to get the machine to surpass the speed of light. Meanwhile, Dr. Motuo continued to pour resources into developing equipment to block the magnetics signals to get the necessary information to thwart his rival's efforts to conquer the impossible dream before him. Just when it seemed success was within reach, the next day would bring new conditions in Dr. Wojcik's laboratory - a variable he couldn't control or predict, frustrating his scientists' progress now involved in a race towards breakthrough technology.

Determined to emerge victorious in the ongoing battle, Dr. Motuo made a bold decision to pour all of his resources and efforts into one final attempt to break through the trenches of his undeclared adversary. His fervent pursuit was so intense that it resulted in the destruction of the entire city's electrical system and all signal-transmitting antennas for cell phones within the designated zone.

The once bustling sector was now plunged into darkness, devoid of any electricity, and all means of communication - including cell phones, cable television, and WIFI - were rendered useless by Dr. Motuo's uncalculated actions. The sky above the city glowed with an eerie red hue as fires raged from some damaged infrastructures, a stark reminder of the consequences of uncontrolled desperation.

Panic set in as he realized the gravity of the situation. In order to cover his tracks and avoid being implicated in this catastrophic event, he would have to destroy all of his equipment and dispose of it elsewhere, far from his property. The very thought made his heart race and his hands tremble. His mind raced with possible scenarios - perhaps they would suspect Dr. Wojcik, the man who had initially created the system that had ultimately failed. But David's facility was one of the few places untouched by the disaster, thanks to the audacious actions of his wife, son, and soon daughter-in-law who had designed a fail-safe installation against such errors. As an experienced player in this game, David knew better than to let unforeseen events destroy years of hard work and determination. He had always taken measures to protect himself from potential threats.

Despite Dr. Locus's determined efforts, it quickly became apparent that he would not be able to extract the coveted secrets from Dr. David after all. He had tried every feasible approach at his disposal, but a nagging feeling in his gut told him that his enemy's defenses were impenetrable at this time. The technological complexities involved in creating a teleportation machine proved to be insurmountable barriers for even the most skilled and resourceful scientists. As much as he wanted to continue pressing for getting those secrets, Dr. Locus reluctantly accepted defeat, knowing that the elusive confidential information would remain just out of his reach. His espionage facility felt emptier now, devoid of the excitement and anticipation that had driven him for some time.

Thus, Dr. Locus harshly came to the realization that his enterprise's success still hinged on one crucial piece of information—the knowledge possessed by Dr. David Wojcik. This knowledge was the know-how of sub-nanoparticle transfer, its decomposition at a subatomic level, and the later regrouping of the elements to reconstruct their molecular structure. With it, all their efforts would be worthwhile. Without it, all their efforts would be in vain.

Bali is Not Coming Back Home

As the sun slowly descended below the horizon a day after Bali disappeared from the Hashbuns residence in 2051, a warm glow spread across the sky, painting it in shades of orange and pink over the skies of Toronto. As darkness settled in, the lights only grew brighter. At the same time, the city lights flickered to life, casting a magical aura over the bustling streets. The reflections of light over the clean window glasses and the sleek vehicles, coupled with the street lamps, illuminated the buildings and sidewalks, creating a vibrant display that seemed to dance in rhythm with the night. It was as if the city was putting on a show just for those lucky enough to witness it amidst the sadness of Bali's absence.

119

The two amigos had to pay hotel bellboys to look after Bali at the different hotels where they stayed for the next two days while conducting their business. On the night of the second day, Bali was missing his routine, and Ginger struggled to keep up with him. It was the end of another busy day for the sneak thieves, who went to downtown Toronto to continue their routine actions.

So, that was time to recap the heyday, take inventory, and now take care of a puppy, too. So, he decided to take him for a walk before bed, but he hadn't expected the chaotic prelude and chase that would involve. Wrapping a makeshift strap around his chest, Ginger secured him with knots he had learned as a young scout. As a leash, he put together two wraps of flexible bandages. Even his scout skills were put to the test when Bali had greater strength than the level of elasticity of the elastic bands.

Bali was a small dog, yet his strength and mischievous nature could not be underestimated. "Uffffff!" Ginger sighed wearily as he ran after Bali, who seemed to enjoy his momentary playtime. Ginger's weary sigh echoed through the empty streets, and Bali's excited barks reverberated in the stillness of the night. Despite Ginger's fatigue, he couldn't avoid smiling at his new joyous canine friend.

Finally, Bali came to a stop in an alleyway; his senses focused eagerly on something in the short distance. Curiosity getting the better of him, Ginger cautiously approached Bali and saw what he had been so fixated on: a rare Fijian albino greenish iguana, very similar to the one he saw on the news the day before–although neither of our two friends paid any attention to that special report, only Bali.

"So, little dog, have you 'Found a Friend'? Ginger sarcastically exclaimed. The creature seemed unperturbed by Bali's presence, calmly surveying his surroundings with his bright red eyes. Ginger couldn't believe his luck—stumbling upon such a unique and beautiful animal in the midst of a bustling city. Savoring the moment, he stood there with Bali, admiring the iguana's intricate patterns and graceful movements in awe.

"Wow! Wow! Wow!" Ginger breathed in wonder and excitement. "Who could smuggle such a magnificent specimen? And what would be his value?" he pondered aloud with a mixture of admiration and curiosity for the iguana. Without hesitation, Ginger lunged forward to seize the iguana, thinking only about the money he could get from selling it. Instead, he was met with a fierce blow from the animal's powerful tail. Undeterred, he persisted in his pursuit, only to have the iguana suddenly turn on him and sink his sharp teeth into his left hand. Bali barked furiously at the iguana in response.

"Aiiiiiii!" Ginger cried out in surprise and pain as the reptile's jaws clamped down on his flesh. He quickly recoiled, frantically waving his injured hand to free himself from the not-so-innocuous reptile. Meanwhile, the iguana scurried away nimbly before coming to a halt a few feet (meters) away, staring at Ginger with his small, bright red eyes. Ginger placated Bali by gently stroking his ears as they both stood there, transfixed by the iguana slowly disappearing at the end of the alley. It was an unexpected encounter that would stay etched in their memories forever, a wild oasis amid the unforgiving concrete jungle.

Once returned to the motel, Bali barked fiercely at anyone who passed by the front door of their room. He wasn't used to sounds at night, much less the constant walk of people coming or going around the front door of a room. A concerned guest alerted the motel administration about the disturbance, which brought an unexpected visitor a few minutes later.

"Knock, knock, knock."

"Open the door. It's the Motel Chief of Surveillance," a stern voice demanded. He was a burly man with broad shoulders and stern features. He wore a crisp navy-blue uniform with shining brass buttons and a silver badge on his chest. His large, calloused hands were folded in front of him, and his posture exuded authority.

Bali's frantic barks echoed through the walls of the room, his primal senses on high alert. In the room, Ben and Ginger hastily shoved their stolen goods from the shopping mall into their bags and shoved them deep inside the bathtub.

"I'm coming. Hold on!" Ben snapped, sweat beading on his forehead as he tried to calm the rising panic in his chest.

As Ben's mind raced, he considered climbing out the bathroom window and fleeing from whatever trouble awaited him. Promptly, Ben remembered Bali's incessant barking and realized that the security guard's presence there must not be connected to their misdeeds. He cursed himself for not being more cautious. Besides, the adrenaline fueled his excitement, and he knew that listening to Ginger had clouded his judgment. Now, he was in the dilemma of facing potential consequences, and he didn't know how to escape them without betraying his partner. So, he decided to stay and play along.

"KNOCK, KNOCK, KNOCK."

The knocking grew louder and more persistent. "What's going on in there?" the head of security asked, his tone becoming increasingly impatient.

"Relax, I'm on my way!" Ben snapped back, growing annoyed at the demands. He finally reached the door as Ginger emerged from the bathroom. Bali was clutched in his arms, a bandage tightly wrapped around his left thumb. The guard immediately scolded them for having a pet in their room, stating that it was against the motel policies.

However, after some words of persuasion from Ben and with some bribery and pleading, Ben and Ginger were able to convince him to let Bali stay for the night. Ben quickly voiced his concerns about Ginger's poor judgment the minute the guard left.

"See, Ginger? This is what happens when insisting on bringing that little dog along," Ben chided him as they settled back into their room. "And now you will have to pay for it. I'll be deducting this from your share of our haul."

Later, Ben meticulously re-inventoried the stolen goods and carefully packed them into his two heavy carry-on bags, arranging them to give the impression that they were his personal belongings—in a way. Now, he couldn't afford any suspicion from the motel staff or other guests.

"Silence, doggy," he grumbled at the restless puppy, who got irritated by every little noise in the unfamiliar room. At that moment, Ginger made the decision to take a moment to scope out their surroundings before settling in for the night. He decided to take one last walk around the facility's premises before going to sleep. Ginger improvised another makeshift leash; this time, he used the shoulder straps of his handbag to secure Bali's wriggling. It wasn't ideal, but it was better than what was improvised previously.

As Bali and Ginger stepped out of the room, they were greeted by the sight of four children playing with a soccer ball a few steps away in the parking lot.

One kid spotted Bali and eagerly asked if they could pet him. "What's his name?" the boy inquired, looking up at Ginger with curious eyes.

He hesitated, unsure of the actual name of the puppy he had been calling 'doggy.' To sympathize as he saw the boy's Disney T-shirt featuring Mickey Mouse, he couldn't resist fitting his fake pet's name into the beloved character's moniker. "His name is Mickey," he answered with a smile.

The boy's eyes lit up in amazement as he read Bali's name tag, which bore the name "Bali." "Are you sure, sir?" the boy inquired. "His name tag reads Bali," he added.

"Wow," he exclaimed, clearly impressed by his carelessness. "But back home, I always call him Mickey Bali," Ginger confided with a wink.

After a brief exchange with the friendly children, Ginger knew it was time for some exercise to tire out his energetic companion. He led Bali on a jog around the perimeter of the motel, enjoying the not-too-warm evening air and feeling grateful for this slight reprieve in their hectic lives as petty thieves on the run. Finally, after exhausting a burst of energy, they returned to their room and settled in for much-needed rest. When they arrived there, Ben decided Bali would need to spend the night in the bathroom to minimize the sounds he might hear; he placed a wettish towel in the small opening gap at the bottom of the bathroom door.

Before the sun rose, Ben woke up about six hours after the incident with the security guard. "I can't believe it, but we survived the night," the old man thought when he peaked through the curtain at the front window of their room and saw the clarity that precedes the sun's brightness on the horizon at dawn. The next day dawned, the sun slowly rising and casting its warm glow over the sky.

The first rays of light illuminated the upper layers of the celestial firmament, painting it a soft orange at the base and a pastel blue toward the high skies. The white clouds seemed to be re-touched by a gentle brush, adding to the picturesque scene. Bali, a coincidental-occurrence dog, was already going out with Ginger to take care of his necessities. As Ben stirred awake in their motel room, he heard in the distance the sound of a car approaching the motel. He knew the sound of vehicles with complete human control because they lacked smooth movement, reflected in the sound of the tires touching the pavement when approaching the motel.

Without hesitation, Ben immediately opened the curtain of the front window to see what was happening outside and checked for any potential endangerments in the parking lot. His sharp senses picked up on the presence of police officers heading toward the motel management office.

He quickly called Ginger and said, with a tone of urgency, "You need to come back right now."

No more than two minutes later, Ginger and Bali came back, and Ben told him, "Gather all our belongings and be ready to escape through the back window of the bathroom with Bali, now!"

The police officers' gesticulations made him realize that they could only be investigating reports of missing objects in nearby residences as they had already settled the incident of the dog barking. Thus, they needed to leave before they got caught. Thanks to the old man's instincts, Ginger, Bali, and he got out seven minutes before the police knocked on their bedroom door.

"Knock, knock, knock."

"Open the door. It's the Toronto Police."

"Knock, knock, knock."

"Open the door. It's the Toronto Police." The police officers stood tall and authoritative outside the door. They

126

looked immaculate in their dark blue uniforms, adorned with badges and patches that sparkled in the sunlight. They wore belts with different kinds of cases around their waists, holding various tools and gadgets. They also carried a gun holstered at her left side.

"KNOCK, KNOCK, KNOCK."

A loud, urgent knocking echoed through the door again.

"Open up. It's the Toronto Police, and this is your final warning." The sound broke the silence of the morning at the motel and woke several of the other hotel guests, who looked out their doors to see what was going on.

However, the police had no concrete evidence against them other than parishioners' complaints about constant barking the previous night. Nonetheless, Ben was confident in his judgment that if someone had been looting houses in the neighborhood, they would have sought refuge in a nearby lodging. He wasn't there to witness his accurate hunch, but as expected, one patrol car was stationed at the front entrance while one of the two officers now guarded the back of the motel room.

Ben, well-versed in his trade and always prepared for an escape, had arranged everything the night before to make their way out of the room through the back window and down the hill, leaving no trace behind. This quick thinking gave them a precious 17 minutes before the agents entered the room to search for them and get back into their vehicles with a reasonable action plan. They used this time wisely to steal another semi-autonomous vehicle parked at a meter not far from the parking lot at the motel, and they made their getaway move as fast as possible from the motel.

Ben certainly had become an expert at breaking into popular keyless security systems. These so-called smart key systems were the easiest to crack, thanks to advances in artificial intelligence that allowed repetitive operations to be more than doubled in record time.

With a burst of adrenaline, Ben fumbled with the car door using his miniature computer until it finally opened. They wasted no time jumping inside and speeding off in the opposite direction towards the bullet train station. A couple of miles ahead (3.22 kilometers), the familiar lights of a highway patrol car appeared in the rearview mirror, causing Ben's heart to race even faster. Before they knew it, the patrol car rapidly approached them from behind, closing the gap with lightning speed. Ben and Ginger exchanged worried glances, their thoughts racing as they prepared for the worst. "I think we've been caught," Ben muttered, his voice trembling with fear. He then made the decision to pull over and face whatever consequences came their way. "We'll have to ask for mercy for our misdeeds," he whispered before bringing the car to a stop on the side of the road. As they waited for the inevitable confrontation, the warm air of winter hung heavy with tension and uncertainty.

As the highway patrol car zoomed past them without even a glance, Ben and Ginger let out a collective sigh of relief. "Wow, that was close," Ginger exclaimed with a grin, his breath visible in the chilly air. Another two patrols followed at light speed. Then, Ben carefully started driving again, his knuckles white from gripping the steering wheel tightly. After another five and a half miles, they spotted a commotion up ahead—a young man being escorted away in handcuffs by two police officers. Intrigued, Ben slowed down to get a closer look. One of the highway patrol cars was sleek and polished; its red and blue lights flashed rhythmically to the siren blaring from its roof. Its paint glistens in the sun, reflecting the surrounding landscape and adding to its intimidating presence.

In another patrol car, a trooper officer wore a crisp, dark gray uniform with shiny black buttons. His posture was upright, and his eyes were sharp and focused, taking in everything around him. He sat inside, always alert, with his eyes scanning for any signs of trouble. From what Ben gathered, this young man allegedly stole the car. The vehicle was undoubtedly high-end, far beyond what someone his age would typically own. And as far as Ben could see, there were no signs of drugs or other illegal substances involved. He couldn't stop wondering what led this young man to err in his judgments about the car's selection—learning from other's mistakes.

Moreover, after Ben had thought about the incident, he commented: "I didn't even catch a glimpse or recall that young man as he sped past us, but I was distracted by our escape. Anyway, it was clear that he had been apprehended for stealing the car." At that moment, Ben saw an opportunity to impart a valuable lesson to his partner: "Ginger, one must always think carefully before acting, for the allure of material possessions can blind us to their true worth and our own capabilities." And with those words, Ben concluded his lecture with a knowing look in Ginger's direction.

After Ben believed that Ginger had understood his lesson, this young man made a comment. "That's exactly what happened to Peter, isn't it?" Ginger said. "Which Peter?" inquired Ben. "You know, the one who joined us on our trip to California," replied Ginger. "Oh, Peter?" responded Ben with a sly smile. "Yes, Peter!" confirmed Ginger. "Nope, I don't recall any Peter," joked Ben, chuckling. He was teasing Ginger until the latter became irritated and told him to let it go.

In any case, the young man who got cut didn't look good. The car was now impounded and surrounded by flashing police lights. This should have served as a stark reminder of the consequences of reckless actions. However, as strange as this may seem, Ben and Ginger couldn't see the analogy of how this event also reflects the risk they are subjected to every time they steal a car. They didn't think that this was something that could also happen to them. Deep down, they were wrong; good always triumphs over evil sooner or later.

Ben had barely started driving when Ginger's urgent voice was determined as he quickly replied him, "We need to turn back and wrap up our mission here. We've already acquired a good valuable loot, and every passing minute in this car is like a ticking time bomb until the owners realize it's gone and activate the tracking system within." Ben's expression mirrored his seriousness as he nodded in agreement. "You're right; we should finish this and head home a little earlier." With that, they both agreed to end their excursion in Toronto and return to New York City.

Ben cautiously drove a quarter mile before making a sharp U-turn towards the train station, his eyes constantly scanning the surroundings for any signs of being followed. The road stretched ahead of them, lined with towering trees that seemed to watch their every move. Every sound made them jump, their hearts racing with adrenaline as they were on their way back home.

As they raced toward the train station, Ben couldn't avoid wondering what he was doing. He heard his deceased father's words clearly in the air, telling him: "Don't be foolish… Think about what those people after you are going to do next." The thought of being involved in a high-speed chase with the police sent shivers down his spine. An instant later, it hit him—of course, the train! If anyone were trying to flee, that would be their first choice. And the police officers were undoubtedly aware of this, too.

Ben's determination only grew stronger as they weaved through the congested traffic of a bustling Monday morning. They were, in reality, disrupting the peaceful atmosphere of the early bird workers, those who get up early to go to work before sunrise and the city streets get hot.

"We have to catch these criminals before they can slip away on the train," was the thought of one of the police officers—Ben had made a correct deduction, and his father would indeed celebrate it.

Ben suddenly recalled a memorable moment from a time travel film, in which the actor Michael J. Fox stands before a traffic light in his truck. He immediately looked around to see if he could emulate it. With a sense of urgency and determination, Ben urged a visibly inexperienced young driver to his left in front of the traffic light to push his car to the limit, inciting him to race against his powerful stolen car.

He accelerated the car from a standstill or in neutral, what is also known as a launch. Then he lowered the vehicle window and looked the other driver in the eyes. A mix of thrill and fear was evident in his expression. These challenges were most popular for those who wanted to have it filmed for their social media pages. Luckily for Ben, the inexperienced driver accepted the challenge with a grin between grimaces; his confidence in his vehicle's speed was palpable. So, Ben did his part at the first intersection by darting between cars and ignoring traffic signs, with a rush of adrenaline fueling his actions. Yet, immediately after the second intersection, he let the other driver get ahead at full speed—a sly smile playing on his lips.

The inexperienced young driver asked his friend in the passenger seat to film the charade. However, he got caught up in the rush of adrenaline and excitement, eagerly complied, and sped up even further. His fingers gripped the wheel as if it were the edge of a cliff, his foot pressing down on the accelerator like a heart beating out of control. He was a blur of determination and recklessness, his eyes alight with the thrill of the chase. His two companions held on tightly as they careened through the streets, eventually coming to a stop at the side of the road where they were caught by the police and now were waiting for the police to do their work. As for Ben, he couldn't believe what he had been a part of—a thrilling chase through city streets and getting away as clean as a whistle.

Despite his owners' desperate hope, fate seemed determined to keep Bali from returning home. The criminals' continued success only further diminished any glimmer of a chance for the Hashbuns to be reunited with their beloved pup. It was as if every hurdle they conquered served as a grim warning that Bali was not coming back home. At that moment, it became painfully clear that Bali's return home was very likely only a distant dream.

Seven and a Half Months Earlier

Seven and a half months ago, Dr. Tatiana was looking for a new pet. She searched through multiple websites, and her eyes scanned through various breeds of puppies. Then, she found a website with an array of adorable Corgi puppies that caught her attention. She clicked on the link and was greeted by a collage of photos, each one showcasing the irresistible cuteness of these furry companions. Within a few clicks, she projected the holograms of some puppies to get a better sense of their dimensions and natural look. After several trials, one particular pup stole her heart with his precious face and playful demeanor.

Without hesitation, Tatiana instructed her computer assistant to make an appointment with the puppy breeder for a meet-and-greet with 'Rocky.' The AI Assistant dialed the number listed on the website, and she eagerly waited for someone to pick up the call on the other end.

"Hi!" this is Jeanna from Corgis' Darlings; how can I help you?" "Hello,—she projected her voice to the ceiling where the room's speaker was located. I am calling about one of your new litters listed on your website," she said, trying to contain her excitement. Without any further ado, Tatiana asked: "Is 'Rocky' still available for sale?" "Give just one sec," Jeanna replied.

Tatiana held her breath at the other end as if it would allow the other person to speed up their work. "Ok, …I'm pleased to confirm that Rocky is still available." Tatiana's heart skipped a beat in relief and joy. She breathed a sigh of relief and thanked the breeder's representative. At that moment, she knew she had found her perfect pet and didn't need to search further. The thought of maybe keeping looking until she met him in person rose in her mind. However, her search now seemed unnecessary when she had already found one she liked.

"Yes! So… he is available. Perfect! Let me give you my credit card to pay for a deposit. …Ah, one more question, Jeanna. When can I meet him and later pick him up?" The anticipation of finally getting to meet Rocky was palpable in Tatiana's voice.

Thus, Tatiana wrote all the information and asked her computer assistant to buy two plane tickets to Jefferson City in two weeks. Tatiana found out that Air Canada had a direct flight from Toronto to Jefferson in only two hours. No matter the extra price for the last-minute purchase, she did not hesitate to buy round-trip tickets for herself and her daughter Katherine.

Tatiana eagerly turned to her mother, Dr. Enilda, seeking guidance in her decision to adopt the dog. She dialed her mother's hologram number but turned to video conferencing instead, as the image projection was too blurry. "What do you think of this photo of Rocky?" she asked with a playful grin, knowing her mother's adoration for canines.

Finally, her mother's smiling face appeared on the screen, filling Tatiana with warmth and comfort. "I believe Rocky would make a wonderful addition to your family, my dear," her mother replied with a tone of certainty. "And he looks absolutely gorgeous in that picture."

A wave of relief washed over Tatiana as she nodded, grateful for her mother's approval. She knew deep down that Rocky was her ideal furry companion, especially with her passion for pampering and hugs. With renewed determination, she completed the plans to bring Rocky into their lives and create countless memories together.

A few days later, on a warm winter afternoon, Tatiana left the office early and surprised her granddaughter, Elena. She called her dad and asked for permission to take her to her home for the afternoon. Tatiana talked to her about Rocky, and both, filled with anticipation, entered Tatiana's room to look at his photos snapshot. The images of this tiny puppy named Rocky, which now adorned the walls, captured Elena's heart the moment she saw them. Tatiana excitedly shared all the characteristics she knew about Rocky. She promised she could play with him every afternoon after school.

After completing her offer to Elena, Tatiana thought seriously about the responsibility of having a puppy or a dog, as they have the exact needs. She looked at Elena tenderly, yet with determined words, she said: "It's important that you learn this from a young age. Loving a dog is not only about playing with and bathing him or her one day. Loving a dog is taking care of him or her every day."

Together, they watched holograms of Rocky, marveling at how lifelike and detailed the images were. Tatiana had saved these precious pictures in her personal cloud, eager for Elena to see them. The girl's eyes sparkled with excitement as her grandmother-in-law spoke of all the adventures they would have together in the yard of the house, where she was going to fill it with toys and doggy installations to have it ready for Rocky before he joined them. Facilities that Bali would, unfortunately, ignore once at the house.

"Grandma, he's so cute! When can we meet him in person?" Elena gushed, unable to contain her excitement any longer.

With a knowing smile, Tatiana replied, "Soon, my dear. Don't worry because he'll be right here with us before you know it."

Elena nodded eagerly and asked, "How many more days until I can hold and play with this adorable little puppy?"

It seemed like the puppy had stolen her heart, too. While looking at the holograms, Elena also noticed some peculiarities about the doggy, and she asked her grandma, "How is it that Rocky has a tail? All the other Corgis I have seen have a round bottom."

"Do not worry, Elena. He will be here soon. Oh! I will ask my friend Mr. Onairam about your question and let you know as soon as I get the answers." (The answer is included at the end of the book).

The two weeks finally passed, and the night before the trip, Tatiana kept explaining to her daughter why she wanted her to travel to Jefferson with her. "It's a simple round trip, honey. We will be home before four in the afternoon, and you can go to your soccer game at five in the afternoon," Tatiana promised her daughter, so she ended the arguments.

"I don't understand why you want me to go if you can go alone. Can you ask Rafik to go with you instead?" Katherine responded to her mother.

"You know how he's so limited in time these days," she answered her daughter. "Honey! Is it to share more time with you, or perhaps… don't you want to share this special moment with your mother?"

Tatiana's husband, Dr. Manuel, arrived. He came home late that night because the operation for which he would provide anesthesia was postponed; instead, he had to wait almost an hour while the nurses prepared the other patient at the hospital.

"Well, Katherine and I are going early tomorrow morning to look for the new puppy," she said excitedly.

"Very well, dear. After losing Mickey last year, I hope the new pet can calm your heart."

"I hope so, Manuel," she replied. Losing Mickey had left a void in Tatiana's heart, and she hoped Rocky would help heal that pain.

The morning of the long-awaited trip to meet Rocky began with a sense of excitement and anticipation. It began like any other day, with Dr. Tatiana rising early to prepare for the journey to Jefferson City. The sun had just begun to peek over the horizon as she bustled about the kitchen, the tantalizing aromas of fresh coffee and toasts filling the air. She took advantage of this rare moment to cook a hearty breakfast for her husband Manuel and their daughter Katherine. With skilled hands, she precisely sliced apples and bananas into bite-sized pieces, knowing that Manuel enjoyed starting his mornings with a refreshing fruit cocktail and a small glass of freshly squeezed orange juice. And for Katherine, she prepared a delectable meal of pan-fried eggs and tender turkey, cooked to perfection in a delicate broth.

Once the savory smells of breakfast filled the air, she turned on the state-of-the-art kitchen television. Instead of a traditional rectangular screen, this futuristic device consisted of a holographic projection that seamlessly blended into its surroundings. With a few simple gestures, viewers could dive into the content and feel fully immersed in what they were watching. It was like stepping into another world, where images danced before her eyes and sound enveloped them in a sensory overload. As the news program began to play, she couldn't help but marvel at how far technology had come in 2050. Everything felt more tangible and alive, creating a truly interactive experience unlike anything she had ever known before.

SmashhhhH... CrashhhhH! Dr. Tatiana suddenly dropped her coffee cup and breakfast plate on the floor. As soon as the commercials ended, the news started with breaking news. To her surprise, she was caught in the news images. This news took her off guard and suddenly she saw pieces of bricks, tin cans and even a Labrador retriever sucked up by an EF 4.5 magnitude tornado.

"What's going on?" Dr. Manuel asked, running out of the bedroom. Katherine also went to the kitchen without wasting any time and asked: "What's wrong, Mom?" As soon as the two arrived in the kitchen, their doubts were dispelled, as they too found themselves immersed in the images of the terrible tornado that had just hit the city of Toronto, causing millions of dollars in losses.

As per the news anchor the storms resulted from a significant amount of atmospheric instability in an environment conducive to powerful thunderstorms, caused by a strong cold front passing through in the mist of winter. Quoting the original survey report from NOAA, "the takeaway from the outbreak is that major tornadoes can occur regardless of location or terrain if the atmospheric conditions are right."

Sixty-five years ago, in the midst of a hot and humid summer on August 14th, 1985, Toronto was struck by a similar monstrous tornado - an event that left a very unpleasant mark on the history of the city. Like the one of six decades ago, this tornado with force and fury, it tore through the city, leaving behind a path of devastation. From shattered windows and crumbled buildings to uprooted trees and debris-strewn streets, the damage was extensive. In the aftermath, authorities deemed it necessary to enforce a curfew for all residents of Toronto as a precautionary measure to protect against any potential dangers that may still linger in the wake of the destructive tornado.

In the aftermath of the devastation, it took over seven grueling days to even begin cleaning up the wreckage. Mountains of debris and rubble filled every corner, a somber reminder of the destruction that had ripped through the region due to climate change. In response, the Ontario provincial government acted swiftly and decisively, releasing emergency funds to aid in the restoration those affected in such thriving community. And with the support of both the Senate and House of Commons, additional resources were allocated to assist all those who had been affected by this natural disaster. It was a race against time, but the determination and resilience of the people would ultimately prevail in rebuilding their beloved home.

Finally, after twelve days after the tornado, flight restrictions were lifted and it was time for Dr. Tatiana and Katherine to go on their trip to meet Rocky. The journey to Jefferson City was a long one for Katherine because it was a trip she didn't want to take to begin with. On the contrary, Tatiana was filled with excitement at the thought of meeting her new Corgi, Rocky. The next day, as they stepped off the electric plane and into the sweltering heat, they were immediately hit with a wave of humidity that made them sweat their undergarments.

The air in Jefferson was thick and hot, the sun beating down mercilessly on the small town. The walls of the airport terminal were lined with solar panels, which, at some angles, allowed the harsh sunlight to stream in and cast a glaring light over everything. The sound of the central air conditioning fans humming and people sweating dampened all their clothes as if they had stepped out of a sauna.

When the travelers left the terminal, they anxiously waited for their taxis or other public or private transport systems. Their eyes were drawn to the news reports flashing across the screens about the heat wave devastating the region. Outside the terminal, the sweltering heat showed no signs of relenting, adding to the somber atmosphere within the airport. Despite the unbearable heat, they were determined to meet Rocky. Tatiana actually couldn't wait to meet her little ball of fur.

Outside the terminal and away from the air conditioning system, the airport in Jefferson also installed humidifiers with tiny water sprinklers in the exit corridors, the transportation waiting areas, and indoor parking areas to ease the intense heat outside the terminal. However, as soon as passengers stepped outside, they were greeted with a sweltering sauna-like atmosphere and immediately drenched in sweat under the scorching sun. Umbrellas had never been so necessary in human history. So, they bought two parasols to protect themselves from the ardent sun.

There in Jefferson, at the Missouri State Penitentiary, the news was broadcasting on the TVs inside the airport of the inevitable hospitalization of twenty-seven inmates because of the intense summer heat—seven of them in intensive care due to severe dehydration. Even so, they were not going back; Tatiana and now Katherine couldn't stop thinking about their future furry family member. They finally arrived at Jefferson, and the imminent anticipation only increased their emotions of meeting the puppy.

On the ride to meet Rocky, the two chatted animatedly about what name would suit him best. After much discussion, they looked at his picture and considered a name that encompassed his personality. Katherine finally agreed to her mother's suggestion of "Billy," although she couldn't resist adding in a nickname of her own—"Bali."

When they finally arrived at the breeder's home, Rocky greeted them with his boundless energy and curiosity. Luckily, the facility had a splendid air conditioning system. Rocky was almost six weeks old, full of enthusiasm, wiggling around with his curious eyes shining and his small, wet black nose twitching. Tatiana noticed something that she hadn't seen before. It wasn't visible in any of the photos or notes on the internet. Bali had a little pink marking on his left lower lip. There was nothing to worry about, the breeder said.

As Dr. Tatiana held him in her arms, she immediately connected with this playful puppy. The little puppy in Tatiana's arms squirmed and licked her face, his tail wagging furiously. She chuckled at the sheer delight in his eyes and whispered, "Alright, little one, looks like you've found yourself a home." With a determined glint in her amber eyes, she glanced over Katherine, who was looking at her with raised eyebrows. "Looks like we have a new family member," Tatiana said, her eyes sparkling with mischief. She knew taking him home would come with challenges and responsibilities, but she was well-prepared and ready to tackle them.

Tatiana and her daughter Katherine were amazed at playing with the Corgi puppy Rocky. Tatiana also took the time to observe his behavior, energy, and zest for life. At that moment, Tatiana knew he would be more than just a pet; he would become her loyal companion. With her decision made, Tatiana spoke confidently with the breeder about shipping Bali to her at a time that she considered prudent.

After carefully checking and signing each document requested by the breeder, Dr. Tatiana pulled out her cell phone and looked for her wallet application to pay for the doggy and services. Her daughter squealed beside her, already planning for their new furry addition to arrive at their home. With relief and excitement, they walked back to their rental car, ready to drive back to the airport. As they drove, the mother couldn't stop smiling, knowing that their new furry addition soon would be reunited with them at his new home.

Seven and a Half Months Later

Seven and a half months had passed since Bali came to the Hashbun's home, and now no one knew much of his whereabouts. Thus, without Bali, the elegant residence of the Hashbun family didn't feel truly alive. Zizzo had his own life, and no one knew where he was. He came and went as he pleased, and his food bowl was always ready for whenever he wanted to eat. Plus, his filtered water fountain never stopped working, so he never got thirsty. That was the most significant difference: the cat rarely needed attention, while Bali needed daily attention.

Thus, the deep, consuming grief over the loss of Mickey and now the missing Bali—both beloved members of their family—still hung heavily in the air. The once-bustling house now seemed eerily quiet and empty without their presence. As they gathered around the breakfast table, the silence

145

was so thick that the words were drowned in their lips before they could be pronounced.

Mickey's sudden passing and Bali's disappearance left a gaping hole in Tatiana's life, one that seemed impossible to fill. As a fierce lawyer, she had always fought for justice with unwavering determination. But now, the mere idea of leaving her house seemed insurmountable. Memories of defending clients who had committed unlawful actions haunted her mind, struggling to reconcile their guilt with her role as their defender. Yet, faced with her deep pain and turmoil, Tatiana could not find a way out of sadness. With each heavy step, Tatiana's heart ached, and her eyes burned with unshed tears as she walked through the empty halls of her grand house.

Everywhere she looked, there were reminders of her beloved dog, Mickey, and her precious puppy, Bali. The once vibrant home now seemed cold and lifeless without their bounding energy. Tatiana felt lost and alone in her lavish living room, adorned with expensive furniture and stacks of legal briefs and case files. The absence of her furry companions weighed heavily on her mind, making it hard to focus on anything else. Even the mere thought of opening her laptop and diving into a case felt staggering. Her entire being struggled to come to terms with the sudden loss of two critical figures in her life—her loyal canine friends who had been by her side through thick and thin.

Desperate to find the family's missing pet, the father turned to his daughter with a heavy heart. "What can we do to find him?" he asked, breaking through the oppressive stillness. His words seemed to echo off the walls, a reminder of their fruitless efforts so far.

The mother looked at her daughter with a mixture of sadness and unwavering love in her eyes. "We have done everything we can think of," she said with a deep sigh. We reached out to all our trusted friends and acquaintances and searched every place in the neighborhood. We even hired a private investigator. However, Bali is still missing."

Her love for Bali fueled the young daughter's determination. She remarked, "I am going to print photos of him and post them on every light post within ten blocks in every direction." Despite the slim chance, her parents nodded in agreement, holding onto any shred of hope.

"I will also upload his pictures on all social media platforms and join online communities dedicated to finding lost or missing pets," she continued. While their endeavors may seem minor in the grand scheme, their deep affection for Bali pushed them to attempt any and every solution to bring him back home.

Katherine rallied support from friends and acquaintances to aid her in the search for Bali. Each individual pledged to reach out to at least two others, and soon, their efforts gained momentum. They printed an abundance of posters, and in only twelve weeks, every street corner in Toronto was adorned with a picture of Bali and the phone number of the lead detective working on this case.

About twenty miles apart, the two rascals, Ben and Ginger, and Bali finally arrived at the buzzing bullet train station, a sprawling complex of steel and glass, with the constant hum of trains and the chatter of people filling the air. Ginger's heart sank as he discovered he had lost his ticket. The busy station was brimming with vibrant energy on that Monday morning. The constant movement of people and trains created a jammed atmosphere. The sound of trains coming and going mixed with the echoes of underground trains and buses connected to this transportation system. Desperate to avoid any trouble or confrontation with Ben, he quickly hatched a plan to steal another ticket instead of trying to ask Ben to duplicate his.

With a sly grin on his face, he began scanning the crowds for someone holding a paper ticket—a rare sight in this modern, digital age. Ginger's eyes darted back and forth, taking in every detail of the bustling station, searching for potential targets. Knowing that older folks were more likely to prefer the traditional printed tickets over digital ones, Ginger narrowed his search and started walking toward older people among the sea of rushing bodies. His keen eyes soon landed on an elderly lady, her wrinkled hands clutching onto a worn paper ticket tightly as if it were her most prized possession. However, ten seconds later, she carelessly dropped it in her glittering Kardashian purse without bothering to close it correctly, a perfect opportunity for Ginger's cunning plan.

Meanwhile, Bali, a lively and exuberant dog, bounded through the bustling train station, trying to greet everyone he passed. His wagging tail and joyful demeanor caught the attention of passersby passengers, who couldn't resist showering him with head pats and loin rubs. As his energy radiated outward, it seemed to uplift even the most serious-faced travelers, drawing smiles and laughter from them in return. Bali's role in the distraction was crucial for Ginger, and his playful antics added a touch of fun and mischief to the scene.

While all eyes were on Bali, Ginger moved stealthily through the crowd toward the identified target, the unsuspecting old lady. Using his nimble fingers, he deftly slipped into her purse and retrieved the paper ticket without her noticing anything. A thrill ran through him as he successfully pulled off this act of thievery, and he hurried away with Bali by his side and the stolen ticket in hand, eager to board the train before he could be caught. Ginger couldn't resist to pat himself on the back for his cunningness. "How lucky I am!" he thought to himself with a twisted sense of satisfaction on his lips. He was not of a good character. He took advantage of an elderly lady regardless of whether she could buy another ticket or not.

Minutes later, the aged lady discovered she had lost the ticket. As the minutes mercilessly ticked by, the aged lady's stomach twisted and turned with each passing second. She tore through her purse like a wild animal, frantically searching for the ticket that was supposed to take her on her long-awaited journey. But it was gone - vanished without a trace. A wave of panic threatened to consume her, but she fought it off with all her might. With steely determination, she made her way through the teeming crowds towards the nearest ticket stand, ignoring the curious glances and whispers that followed her.

She silently thanked all the deities in existence for informing her of the loss of her ticket early enough to take corrective action-there was no time to claim the loss of her ticket as there was no time to deal with bureaucracy now. With only ten minutes left until their bullet train's departure, she knew every second counted.

Ginger was still gloating over his feat. Yet, he knew Bali had to relieve himself before boarding the train. So, he took the time to get him outside but now he was the one who was securing his ticket and belongings whenever he goes. A few minutes later the deafening buzz of the station seemed to mock him as he raced against time because Bali got them distracted. At that moment he was weaving through throngs of people like a desperate warrior on a mission. But at last, they reached their train platform with seconds to spare - their hearts racing, lungs heaving, but grateful for no missing the train.

Bali's Memorable Moments

Excitement filled the air as Tatiana and Manuel made their way through the bustling Toronto Airport. They were there to pick up Tatiana's mother, who had agreed to travel all the way from France to spend a few months with them after Bali disappeared from their home. She was a strong woman, but her voice was smooth and warm as melted butter, and her amber eyes seemed to hold all the secrets of the universe.

Dr. Enilda had been a Literature Professor at the University of Poitiers of Paris, France, for almost 30 years. Still, now that she was retired, she occasionally taught courses on technical writing to single students or small companies. Her strength radiated from her being, and she would do anything for her beloved family. After the sudden disappearance of their family dog, Bali, Tatiana fell into a deep depressive state. Therefore, she came to Canada to stay with her daughter and son-in-law and support them in any way possible.

Toronto Airport was a marvel of modern engineering. The peaked steel and fiberglass roofs that used to dominate the landscape had been replaced with sleek, energy-efficient glass structures that harnessed solar power. As they navigated through the terminal, Tatiana and Manuel couldn't stop admiring the remodeling of the biophysical design that incorporated green spaces on each level.

The new airplanes were a marvel of aerodynamics with an incredible electric propulsion system. The electric aircraft bringing Dr. Enilda reached an impressive speed of 910 miles per hour (1,464.50 kilometers per hour). For the distance of 3,726 miles (5,996.42 kilometers) between Paris, France, and Toronto, Canada, the engineering of the aircraft reduced the travel time significantly from the usual 8 hours and 45 minutes in the 2030s to only a little over 4 hours and 12 minutes by the end of 2040s, depending, of course, on the weather.

For Dr. Tatiana's mother, Dr. Enilda, it was a comfortable journey thanks to the modern amenities available on board. The amenities for their premier customers included plush reclining seats that lie back to almost 155 degrees with the woven, modacrylic Linstol's blankets to keep passengers warm and comfortable on board. Also, sparkling clean multiple bathrooms with luxurious hand soaps and a supply of fresh towels instead of paper towels. Soft down pillows, a variety of different kinds of nuts and chips, as well as hot sandwiches, and a never-ending supply of champagne or wine. Not to mention the unlimited coffee, bottled water, and assorted candies. All these luxuries were only available on this high-end airline for their first-class customers, making the journey a comfortable and indulgent experience. So, Dr. Enilda really welcomed this trip not only to spend time with her daughter and to help her deal with her lingering grief over Bali's disappearance but for her own distraction, too.

After the initial welcome hugs, Tatiana turned to her mother with bright eyes and a warm smile. "Oh, Mom, I am so happy to see you! How was your trip?" she asked eagerly.

Manuel joined in, wrapping his arms around his mother-in-law and planting a kiss on her cheek. "Welcome to Toronto, Enilda! I hope everything went smoothly," he said warmly.

Enilda beamed at her daughter and her loving gestures. "Yes, everything was wonderful! Thank you both for inviting me to stay at your lovely home." Suddenly, her face grew serious as she remembered something. "Now, refresh my mind. How did Bali escape from the patio?" Enilda asked.

Tatiana and Manuel exchanged glances before Tatiana spoke up. "We're not sure yet; we've hired a highly reputable detective to help us find him. He's been reviewing all the security cameras in the area and waiting for approval from a city council to access drone images that may help locate him."

Enilda, who had been listening quietly, finally spoke up. "It's amazing how advanced technology is these days. Truly impressive." She smiled proudly at her daughter and son-in-law for taking swift action. "I am well aware of how much your granddaughter, Elena, cares for this puppy. I truly hope the detective can retrieve him soon," she concluded.

The Hashbun's house was filled with warmth and laughter as Manuel, Tatiana, Katherine, Rafik, Enilda, and Elena gathered for dinner. The aroma of exotic spices and cooking meat wafted through the air, making stomachs growl in anticipation. Dr. Enilda arrived in Toronto with some Parisian sweets, adding to the lively atmosphere of the gathering. The group was already seated at the main table, their mouths watering at the sight of the perfectly cooked cultured meat prepared by Tatiana.

Even Dr. Enilda couldn't resist complimenting the stir-fried seaweed in sesame oil. As they ate, Rafik and Elena eagerly tried the rice topped with insects, those delicious escamoles (ant larvae), and allergen-free nuts. Manuel's pinto beans stole the show with rich flavors enhanced by ham, cassava, zumitam potatoes, Mexican squash, carrots, coconut oil, and his secret ingredient—a medley of green vegetables as seasoning. Finally, the time for dessert—a superb cold walnut cake paired with warm ginger tea and milk. As they savored each bite, they reminisced about their favorite memories of living with Bali, their voices filled with joy and nostalgia.

After dinner, a distant dog's bark caught everyone's attention straight away. They all got up from the table and rushed to the backyard, eager to find the source of the sound. They heard another bark, this time coming from the front of the house. The group quickly shifted to the front, but there was no sign of a puppy anywhere.

Elena felt confused and asked, "How can this be possible? How is this happening?" Elena was puzzled. " I heard those Bali barks like coming from nowhere or everywhere."

After the mesmerizing experience of hearing Bali's barks, the explanation was now in question. Dr. Rafik's sharp memory brought back a public television broadcast about sounds, and he said, "As the sun sets, the temperature inversion allows sound waves to travel further horizontally. The calmer atmosphere at night also reduces wind disturbances, making sounds more audible over greater distances than in daytime. Thus, this sound could be from any other dog."

However, Katherine immediately rebutted him, "You are coming to conclusions too fast, brother. Researchers have proven that each dog has his own unique pitch or tone to his bark."

"So, were those Bali's barks or not?" Elena asked.

"Unfortunately, we'll never know that," Katherine concluded.

"Very well, sister, you made a good observation this time," Dr. Rafik relented.

Eventually, they gave up and returned inside, trying to make sense of what just happened. Then Tatiana decided to put on some dog music that came to mind at that moment. She set up the stereo in the living room and adjusted the surround sound system for a better experience. She selected the song "Chasing Butterflies" by Jordon Frank. It's a classic country oldies song that was on the air in early 2016. As soon as the song started playing, Tatiana got very emotional.

From the song's first note, her features contorted in a mix of grief and disappointment. She couldn't help her emotions as the song reminded her of what she said to Dr. Manuel about her missing puppy: "From the moment I laid eyes on Bali, I knew I had to bring him home with me." Then, she felt a lump in the throat and contracted her eyes, as did her nose and mouth, in a twist of sadness. Then, it was palpable when traces of tears began to form in her eyes.

As the rest of them sat in the living room, still perplexed by the inexplicable sound, they turned to Tatiana, who suddenly started crying. The rest of the group joined in, one by one. Their tears were a manifestation of their shared helplessness. Their cries and tears filled the room and wet the floor with pools of tears. Realizing how soaked their shoes had become, they took them off to dry outside, symbolizing the end of inertia and their need to move beyond powerlessness and find some confidence. But after discovering that even their socks had become drenched in tears, they removed them, leaving everyone barefoot and in despair. On a good note, the marble floor of the living room, instead of being cold, had been warmed by weeping tears, as had their hopes to find Bali.

They all huddled together that night in the cozy and spacious Hashbun residence, finding comfort in each other's presence. The old wooden floors of the second floor creaked beneath their footsteps as they made their way to the bedrooms, which were adorned with quaint decor and soft, inviting beds. As the night deepened, Tatiana tossed and turned in bed, her mind restless with thoughts about the mysterious sounds the family had stumbled upon earlier that night. The moon's silver light filtered through the curtains, casting eerie shadows on the walls of her room.

The floorboards groaned softly beneath her weight as she tiptoed to the window, pushing it open to let in the cool night air. Unable to shake off the pull of emptiness, she returned to bed, hoping to find internal peace. Her husband, Manuel, stirred from his slumber on the other side of the king-size bed, sensing Tatiana's restlessness. Manuel got up and padded over to Tatiana's side with a soft movement, caressing her hand reassuringly. After that, they couldn't find their way back to sleep and went to the kitchen for a cup of tea. There, they spent the entire night talking about the trivialities of life and how much they missed Mickey and Bali. Before sunrise, they took a refreshing bath and returned to the kitchen to prepare breakfast for their guests.

That following morning, around 7:51 AM, a delicious aroma with a mixture of coffee, tea, and hot chocolate filled the air as everyone gathered around the warm kitchen breakfast table. The sun shone through the windows, casting golden rays on the smiling faces of all the family members gathered there. Laughter and chatter filled the room as they enjoyed a hearty breakfast together, grateful for the warmth and hospitality of their hosts.

During breakfast time, some indulged in a rich, creamy chocolate drink, while others preferred the bold flavors of an Arabic coffee paired with freshly baked homemade cookies. While the group was enjoying the delicacies of the meal, Tatiana brought a little more of her nostalgia after seeing the photo of Bali in the living room. Her mom, Enilda, got close to her and told her: "What we love the most never leaves us. It will always live in our memories and our hearts." Katherine couldn't avoid hearing what Dr. Enilda said, and she immediately added: "Mom, let the memories of Bali bring you comfort during this time of sorrow, please."

Tatiana's arms welcomed Katherine in a lovely hug, holding onto her for a few moments before nuzzling her to the side. She brushed aside the strands of hair that obscured Katherine's face, revealing her tear-stained cheeks and quivering lips. Then, a heavy sigh escaped Tatiana's lips as she struggled to contain her overwhelming emotions before finally telling her close to her ears: "I understand, don't worry. It's just that Bali had everything he needed here. I cared for his food, bath, short walks, and vet visits. I bought him all the treats he liked. I played with him in the yard and walked together in the nearby parks. Now he's out in the city, and I'm sure no one will care for him like I did. That hurts me the most because Bali is my little baby."

As the group reminisced about Bali's early days, Tatiana's voice cut through the warm morning air of winter. "Do you remember when we first let Bali play with Zizzo? Yes, our two-and-a-half-year-old cat," she asked with a smile.

The reply was unanimous—everyone remembered that fateful day. "Zizzo almost pierced his right eye," chimed in Rafik solemnly. "Yet he was saved by the thin hair of a flea," as Grandma Enilda always said.

As the conversation continued, Katherine revealed that their time with Bali had transformed Zizzo from a simple house cat into a breathing creature sloping that pup just like them. Bali would run around him, and the two would play, sometimes like cats and others like dogs. In addition to Bali learning to jump, Zizzo learned to come and have breakfast with everyone in the kitchen.

"Get out!" Elena's voice crashed through the chatter as she scolded Zizzo for attempting to climb onto the table—he was still with his paws on the windowsill. Elena took a bite of the red, deliciously fragrant salmon baked in parchment paper, mixed with citrus and vegetables, and drizzled with olive oil. It was Zizzo's favorite dish, although he wasn't allowed to eat it.

Rafik commented two weeks after Bali's arrival, "Elena was determined to spend more time with her grandmother Tatiana's new dog. So, with an air of determination, she begged and pleaded with me, tugging at my arm and using every trick in the book to sway me." So, they all knew the finale.

"After some hesitation, Rafik relented, still unable to resist the longing in his daughter's eyes to grant her wishes," Tatiana added.

"Fine, I'll be picking you up before it gets dark," that is how he finished, Elena riposted. With this ending, a smile played at the corners of everybody's mouths.

Rafik said next, "Elena couldn't contain her excitement as she let out a loud 'Yes!' and raced out the door toward the car. I drove her to Tatiana's house that day, and Elena could hardly sit still. She couldn't wait to see Bali again." "Although, when she tried to get Bali to come with her for a walk down the road, he refused to budge. Instead, he sat motionless and sniffed at the ground before attempting to run back toward the safety of the house he had arrived at," concluded Tatiana.

Tatiana expanded, "After much coaxing and gentle words from Elena, Bali finally relented and began walking by her side. His soft, fluffy coat danced in the gentle breeze as he trotted happily, his tail wagging in anticipation of the return home. I remember the sound of his excited barking filling the air, growing louder and more enthusiastic as they approached our home."

Then Manuel was inspired and said, "The scent of freshly cut grass and blooming roses welcomed them as they drew closer. Bali's excitement was contagious, and Elena couldn't avoid smiling at the joyful energy radiating from her furry companion."

Rafik joined the conversation, "As soon as Elena opened the door, Bali came bounding toward her with uncontainable joy. His tail wagged so hard that his entire body seemed to shake with happiness. Elena kneeled down, and Bali jumped into her arms, showering her face with slobbery kisses."

In only three short months, Bali had grown at an astonishing rate. He was already nearly half the size of a fully grown Corgi in both weight and size. Despite his growth, he maintained the curious nature of a puppy, always eager to explore, observe, sniff, and nibble at everything around him. By playing with his feline companion Zizzo, he learned valuable skills such as closing his eyes when she approached to play fight with him and effectively immobilizing her by securing one of her back legs. His shyness about walking had disappeared, and by six months old, he was already darting around the house's patio with boundless energy.

Katherine also shared her experience with Bali when she invited friends to study at her house. As she opened the front door, it was as if Bali eagerly awaited her signal and burst out like a bullet. "Where are you going?" she called after him in amusement. In a matter of minutes, he had scampered about half of a quarter mile (201.16 meters) away from the house and into the adjacent street. Frantically, Katherine had to run after him and call for her mother's help. Tatiana quickly sprang into action and alerted the police in case anyone found him.

Thankfully, Bali had stopped in front of a nearby house where he was happily being petted by the owner of a gentle Cocker Spaniel. It seemed like his hormones were already kicking in, causing him to wander off in search of other furry friends. When he finally heard Katherine's voice calling for him, he came bounding back to her side. He was showing uncontainable joy.

— — —

No one commented on certain things that lie in the collective memories of those who had gotten to know Bali.

At seven months old, Bali ruled the house with an iron paw. He would wake up first, and his barks demanded breakfast until the rest of the household had to wake up early, including Sundays. And not any ordinary breakfast, no—Bali was served salmon croquettes adorned with tiny turkeys cut in pieces, his favorite indulgence.

Also, in this household, Bali's food took precedence over everyone else's. It was prepared before anyone else's meal, ensuring that Bali had ample time to finish and go outside to take care of business before the others left for their daily duties. The Hashbun family may have paid for cleaning service three times a week, yet it was only for the ground floor and bathrooms. The rest of the house was left to the care of the other family members because Bali and Zizzo only counted on dirtying it even more.

One day, while Bali was alone with the cat Zizzo, a dispute broke out over a toy. Bali was not one who welcomed sharing his belongings, especially not his toys. In a fit of rage, Zizzo snatched one toy and retreated to the safety top of a reclining sofa, dropping it probably inside of it. At that moment, Bali was not to be deterred. He pawed a hole in the back of the couch to retrieve his precious possession. When he couldn't find it, his anger only grew, and he proceeded to destroy the entire interior of the sofa until only its frame remained.

Dr. Manuel arrived from work earlier than the rest of the family on that day because he had a canceled operation. As soon as he saw the destruction wrought by his mischievous puppy, he was tempted to lock him in his travel cage as punishment. "What on earth have you done, Bali?" he exclaimed in frustration.

But there was no use scolding him now; instead, he donned jeans and a T-shirt and began picking up and discarding the ruined pieces of furniture. In the end, all that remained of the once-comfortable sofa were scraps and memories of Bali's destructive wrath. Dr. Manuel could only shake his head and sigh, wondering what other chaos his beloved Bali would cause next.

— — —

Other Bali's memorable events not mentioned...

Tatiana called Bali for breakfast one morning, one or two months after his arrival.

"Bali... Bali... Bali! Come on, come here."

Seeing that he did not respond, she had to ask her husband and daughter if they knew where he was. Katherine called Rafik to help her look for Bali. Later that morning, Manuel, Tatiana, Rafik, Katherine, and Elena went out to look for Bali in every direction. A couple of hours later, they returned home breathless and frustrated at not having found him. They didn't stop looking until the end of that day. They had supper at Tim Hortons before heading back home. The sun was setting, slowly casting a warm orange glow over the neighborhood as they trudged back to their house.

Upon their arrival home, Tatiana sat at the kitchen table. The 'help' was about to leave, yet she decided to bake something for them. Taiana's hands shook as she wrote a note

164

for the police. The scent of freshly baked cookies filled the air, even though none of them could bring themselves to eat. Suddenly, the doorbell rang, jolting them out of their thoughts.

"Who is it?" Rafik asked anxiously.

"It's our neighbors from down the street," Katherine replied as she approached the door and saw their faces in the doorbell camera.

"Open it for them!" Rafik urged.

"I'm coming!" Katherine called back, a hint of irritation in her voice. "Ohhh, it's Bali!" Katherine exclaimed as she opened the door to reveal their enthusiastic neighbor with their young boy in tow.

"Hello, neighbors! We've stopped by here three times already, but no one ever answered the door," the neighbor cheerfully explained. It turned out that Bali had gone off to play with the neighbors' four-year-old son, enchanted by his contagious energy and curiosity. The Hashbuns couldn't figure out if the side door for the garbage disposal was open or if their fence had a hole in it somewhere.

Relief flooded over Tatiana and Manuel as they welcomed their neighbors into their home. They spent the evening catching up on each other's lives while Bali and their child ran around, playing games and laughing together. Despite all the anguish and the hustle and bustle over their new family member's disappearance for a brief moment, all was well in this little corner of the world.

The month before Bali visited their neighbors, Dr. Manuel enjoyed having his granola and creamy vanilla yogurt breakfast. He took a bite, and a sharp pain shot through his tooth, causing him to wince and feel discomfort. His busy schedule had caused him to neglect his dental health, and now he would have to face the consequences. Carefully inspecting his teeth, Manuel noticed slight bleeding from his lower left dental implant on tooth number 19. Feeling anxious, he quickly picked up his phone and dialed the dentist's office where he had the implant done.

"Hello! I have an emergency with my dental implant, and I would like to make an appointment with Dr. Slatkin as soon as possible," he explained in a hushed voice. "Sure, take your time. I'll wait here in line."

After a brief pause, the receptionist replied, "I found your record. It has been a while since your last visit," she said.

"Well, I rarely go to the dentist, maybe every other year, for a cleaning," Dr. Manuel said in a rebuttal.

"Is Wednesday at 1:45 p.m. a good day and time for you?" the receptionist asked.

"Yep, that's fine." The receptionist then scheduled his visit to the dentist clinic in Cheektowaga, New York.

Despite being 20 years since his implant surgery, Manuel had always put off going back because of his demanding work schedule and frequent trips to Europe.

"Tatiana, we have to go to Buffalo, NY," he announced after making the dentist's appointment.

Excitedly, she replied, "Perfect! I can't wait! Because I am also planning on ordering new curtains while we're there."

"That's Good. I saw a beautiful design by Levalor on their website that would look perfect in our room," Manuel added with a smile.

As they hurtled down the highway, their speedometer ticking off each passing mile mercilessly, Manuel's eyes widened in terror as he realized his grave mistake. They had already driven about 12 miles (19.31 kilometers) when Manuel realized he had forgotten his passport while mentally inventorying what was needed to cross the immigration post to the United States.

He frantically searched through all his pockets, throwing little receipts and folded papers aside in a mad frenzy, but his passport was nowhere to be found. The realization sunk in like a weight on his chest—they were nearing midway to the immigration post, and he was without the one document to make or break their journey. "Baby, I forgot my passport at home," he told his wife.

Tatiana's eyes widened in disbelief as Manuel's careless confession hung in the air. Bali, their loyal doggy, lifted his head and thumped his tail against the car seat, sensing the tension between his owners. Without a word, Tatiana whipped the car around and sped back toward their house. The silence inside was heavy and thick, like an invisible barrier between them. Bali observed curiously through the window as they turned around in a U-turn, exactly where a sign prohibited it.

They were back home after driving another fourteen minutes in the opposite direction. Manuel wasted no time and rushed to the kitchen, frantically searching the cluttered counter for his passport. The sound of drawers opening and closing echoed through the quiet house. He suddenly exclaimed, "I found it." He dashed back to the electric vehicle, where Tatiana sat impatiently waiting. With a determined look on her face, she stepped on the gas, and they were off again, racing toward the border with the United States.

Both Tatiana and Manuel carried a heavy burden of responsibilities in their respective careers. As a lawyer, Tatiana must meet all her client deadlines at the law office. At the same time, Manuel couldn't miss an operation at the hospital without a valid reason—the hospital would suffer financial losses by having to reschedule surgeries. Thus, missing another day to deal with this issue would inconvenience them if they could not cross the border in due course to make it to Manuel's appointment on time. Hence, with Bali's head sticking out of the passenger side window, they were a team willing to do anything to reach their destination on time. Tatiana took manual control of the car and didn't follow all the speed regulations as the cruise control would have done. As they zoomed down the highway, Tatiana couldn't resist letting out a sigh of relief—they were in this together, and nothing could delay them now.

The silence in the car turned suffocating as Tatiana pushed the speed higher, her grip on the wheel tight and determined. Bali sat in the back seat, his gaze flickering with curiosity at the flurry of movement inside their sleek 2049 semi-autonomous electric vehicle. The windows were now shut tight, trapping their breath and body heat inside, no matter if the air conditioner was running at total capacity.

As they raced back to the border to the USA, the blazing winter sun beat down upon them, and its scorching rays bounced off the watery surface of the road, creating a glaring mirage that danced before their eyes. The heat was almost intolerable that morning, but Tatiana remained focused on getting them to her husband's dental appointment as quickly as possible, no matter the obstacles. Manuel could feel beads of sweat forming on his forehead as he watched the passing landscape blur together in a hazy heatwave.

Eventually, they made it on time for Manuel's dental appointment, thanks to Tatiana. She hesitantly left Manuel at Dr. Slatkin's dental office, still curious about what was truly happening to him. He always seemed guarded about discussing his personal issues. After dropping him off for his appointment, she went to do some errands during the hour or so the dentist offered Manuel to fix the problem. So, first, she wanted to visit Galleria Mall and second, Lowe's, the home improvement store.

His first errand was to buy new shoes for Elena's birthday since there were always specials in Walden Galleria. This mall survived the ravages of time thanks to the creative ability of the managers. They included some office spaces and others for interactive recreation to include the digital experience for their clientele. In addition to their virtual reality options when purchasing large machinery and equipment. The top management also adjusted their physical structure to save money with renewable resources. They installed solar panels on the roofs and more trees in the commercial area to meet the Environmental, Social, and Governance demands.

She made it to Walden Galleria in less than ten minutes. When she arrived, she started walking quickly with Bali on her leash to DSW, where shoes are always offered at a reasonable price. On her way to the store, Bali suddenly stopped to pee in the middle of the aisle. She looked around to see if anyone had noticed, and when she didn't see anyone, she decided to keep going because time was not on her side. "The cleaners will take care of it," she thought.

However, about three stores ahead, Bali stops again. This time, he made a different kind of request for the stop. One of the employees at the store where this happened gave Tatiana a dirty look, and she immediately replied, "Of course

I'll clean it." Luckily, she always carried napkins and small black plastic bags in her handbag for her dog's emergencies. She cleaned it up, looked at the time, and then decided to leave the shoes for another day since she still had to order new curtains. She quickened her pace, left the mall, and quickly headed to her next destination.

Tatiana couldn't shake the feeling of unease that had settled in her stomach since they arrived. She took her pink pills and drank water from her little bottle. "Maybe it's all because of the stress," she thought. As she walked through the sliding doors of the home improvement store, she immediately made her way to the 'Home Decor' section, where she had dealt with the friendly Ms. Nancy for years. Besides, she recalled the candies she kept on her desk and considered how savoring one might help ease the heaviness in her stomach.

Once Tatiana stepped in, Sales Specials' signs hung everywhere, and the hallway was filled with Christmas items on sale and decorations. The holiday spirit was in full force, with festive ornaments on every corner and sales signs beckoning from every angle, creating a lively and bustling atmosphere. Tatiana exchanged pleasantries with Ms. Nancy before placing an order for new curtains. Nancy quickly took her order and got their order in the system. Then, they spent a few more minutes chatting about inconsequential topics before Tatiana finally decided to explore another store section—If she still had time.

Meanwhile, back at the dental office, Dr. Manuel explained to Dr. Slatkin Jr. about his father's previous implant, which had ruptured after twenty years. Dr. Slatkin Jr. carefully examined him and instructed him to wait a few minutes for his father's arrival. The elder Dr. Slatkin appeared, yet he didn't seem to remember Dr. Manuel at all. Despite this, his professionalism overrode any personal feelings, and he treated Manuel appropriately and provided excellent service.

As Tatiana waited for the gallon of a paint color, she ordered to be prepared, her attention was drawn to a commotion coming from another aisle. Bali, her mischievous puppy, had inadvertently slipped out of his collar and was now darting around the store, playfully chasing another dog. In his excitement, he tripped over one of the shelves in the hallway, causing a domino effect throughout the small section filled with Christmas decorations in front of 'Home Décor.' The sound of shattering glass echoed through the store as Mrs. Nancy watched in shock and surprise. The Assistant Manager, Mr. Keith, came quickly to see what was going on. Other nearby associates also went to this store section to see what happened.

Tatiana quickly realized that Bali was to blame for what had happened and immediately chased after him, pulling him back and putting him on a leash again. However, instead of scolding the guilty furry canine, Mrs. Nancy's expression softened into a smile as she watched Bali scamper around innocently amid the chaos he had created. She reached into her pocket and pulled out a puppy treat, offering it to Bali with a kind and understanding gesture. Tatiana couldn't avoid forcing a smile at the scene before her, grateful for Mrs. Nancy's patience and kindness toward her mischievous pup. Tatiana offered to clean up the mess, but Mr. Keith told her not to worry. He and the other associates gathered there would have to clean up everything Bali had destroyed.

With an ashamed face, Dr. Tatiana decided to end her visit to Lowe's. Then, she went to the dental clinic to pick up her husband. As they entered the reception area, Bali somehow managed to wander off and get lost again. With a heavy heart, Dr. Tatiana left her seat and set off in search of Bali. Her cheeks were flushed with shame as she remembered the chaos that had ensued at the home improvement store. She had forgotten to secure Bali's collar properly, and he had started to wreak havoc on the clinic, darting through the hallways and startling patients and dentists alike. The once peaceful clinic was now a scene of chaotic screams and overturned chairs.

Dr. Tatiana frantically chased after Bali, feeling the disapproving glares of every person in the room. She called out his name, but he seemed determined to continue his wild rampage through the installation, leaping over furniture with surprising agility. When Tatiana thought all hope was lost, her husband Manuel appeared at the end of the hallway, looking bewildered as he saw his wife chasing Bali.

Amid the pandemonium, Manuel relievedly chuckled and joined in on the pursuit, laughing while chasing Bali. The other patients and staff watched in amazement as the couple ran into each other in a chasing game worthy of being filmed for TikTok. In the end, Manuel managed to catch Bali before more damage could be done.

As they finally made it back to their car, Dr. Tatiana and Manuel exchanged a knowing glance. "Perhaps we should stick to a less playful pet," they joked to each other. Deep down, they couldn't help but feel grateful for the excitement and joy that Bali brought into their lives—even if it came at unexpected times like this one.

So, now that Manuel's teeth were perfect, thanks to the new teeth-in-a-day technology, he proposed to Tatiana to eat buffalo wings at the new Anchor's Bar that opened inside Walden Galleria. This franchise's first location is a bar restaurant founded in 1935. This particular bar gained popularity for its claim to have invented spicy chicken wings, known worldwide as Buffalo wings. Of course, she agreed without thinking twice since, this way, she could kill two birds with one stone. Enjoy the delicious food at the restaurant and then buy Elena's shoes.

Bali Escaped

To Another Dimension

Looking back, approximately seven and a half months ago, the Hashbuns got a new puppy. However, one must go a little further to unravel the warmness in the events surrounding the story of Bali's arrival at this residence for the first time. Thus, let's go nine and a half long months back since the traumatic event that still haunted Dr. Manuel Hashbun MD and his family. The Hashbun family will never forget when their beloved dog Mickey was hit by a non-autonomous vehicle. According to the police report, it was not the driver's fault since the dog ran away from his owners and slipped into the road in front of the park where they had taken him for a walk.

Despite the heart-wrenching loss of their puppy, the family's resilience shone through as they decided to find another one two and a half months later. Approximately seven and a half months ago, at seven o'clock at night, they embarked on their journey to the airport—Dr. Hashbun, his wife, Dr. Tatiana, and their precious daughter Katherine. The bustling city streets slowly faded into the background as their electric semi-autonomous sedan joined the stream of cars on the highway leading to the airport.

As they merged onto the highway, a sudden shriek of tires and a blinding flash of headlights cut through the peaceful evening air. A car hurtled toward them at an alarming speed, threatening to crash into their vehicle. Evidently, the other driver was speeding, as Manuel exceeded the speed limit by seven miles per hour right after entering the highway.

In a split second, Dr. Manuel Hashbun's instincts kicked in, and he took control of the car, swerving sharply to avoid a collision with the oncoming vehicle. With a loud "thud," their car slammed into the crash barriers, sending shockwaves through their bodies. Seven other automobiles got involved in this small-scale collision on the highway.

Dr. Hashbun's heart pounded in his chest, the adrenaline coursing through his veins as he sprinted toward his family. His hands trembled as he took in their shaken hands but, thankfully, in unharmed states. The chaotic scene around them was a sensory overload—blaring horns, people calling for help, and others screaming at each other. Yet, amid the madness, no one else was directly hit by their car. Also, the one that almost hit them narrowly missed crashing into another vehicle. It was as if they were standing in the eye of a hurricane, watching the chaos swirling around them while remaining miraculously unscathed. Or maybe it was all because of the fortune of everything coinciding around the luck of the number seven.

"Aaiiiiiiiih!" Tatiana's breath caught in her throat as she clutched her husband's arm with a vice-like grip at the moment they impacted against the crash barrier. Their daughter whimpered in fear, her tiny hand seeking solace from her mother's protective embrace. Amid the chaos and danger surrounding them, Dr. Hashbun's unwavering composure was a beacon of reassurance—his expression reflected years spent training and operating in high-stress situations at the hospital.

"Ri-i-ing! Ri-i-ing! Ri-i-ing." As they were catching their breath and expressing gratitude for narrowly avoiding a collision, Dr. Hashbun's cell phone rang abruptly, its jarring tone cutting through the commotion like a sharp knife. It was a notification from the airline—the cargo flight they were expecting had been delayed by an hour, adding to their already harried journey.

As their car rumbled down the road toward the airport, a mixture of relief and frustration washed over them. The vehicle vibrated with the force of their hearts pounding in sync, a mix of relief and frustration coursing through their veins as they hurtled toward the airport. The scene of the near-fatal accident blurred and faded into the distance, yet the haunting sound of metal crushing against metal still rang loud in their ears. Each family member struggled to calm their racing thoughts, clinging to one another for joy at being alive as they made their way to continue their journey on autopilot.

Every breath felt like a miracle, a reminder of their narrow escape from a tragic collision. Gazing at the passing scenery, tears welled in their eyes as they contemplated how easily everything could have been taken away. So, at this moment, huddled together in the car, the family's bond felt more robust than ever, a renewed appreciation for each other's existence uniting them even more.

Dr. Hashbun's insurance report was a simple matter, as his accident did not involve any other drivers. With a calm and collected demeanor, he contacted the insurance company, reported the incident, and then dutifully notified the police without getting into any arguments with anyone else. Fifty-nine minutes later, they arrived at the bustling airport terminal barely in time to see their expected cargo flight touching down on the tarmac. Excitement bubbled within them all as they eagerly awaited the arrival of that small, precious puppy from Jefferson City, Missouri. Their anticipation was palpable, adding an extra layer of excitement to the air.

The breed of dog they were expecting was none other than a Cardigan Welsh Corgi—an adorable and unique small dog with short legs that originated in Pembroke, Wales, one of the constituent nations of the United Kingdom. It is said that these dogs were favorites of the late Queen Elizabeth II of England, who made them world famous.

As Dr. Hashbun reminisced about the day he brought Mickey home, he couldn't help feeling a pang of nostalgia. He was also mindful of his son and granddaughter's recent departure from their house. Dr. Rafik Hashbun, MD, had decided it was time to branch out on his own and find his own place to live, citing their spoiled granddaughter as the reason for needing some space from her loving grandfather.

"Ploc! Ploc!" As his mind drifted back to memories of his son's departure from home, Dr. Hashbun's cell phone message signal jolted him back to reality. He just missed a call, but thank God for the voicemail service. "Hi, Dr. Hashbun; this is Angely from Air Canada Cargo. I am pleased to inform you that your puppy is ready for pickup at the airline's Cargo counter. Air Canada Cargo is located at Terminal 1 of Toronto Pearson International Airport. Thank you." "Wow! We made it just in time; the puppy is already here!" Dr. Manuel reacted.

As they made their way toward the Cargo terminal, Katherine let out an audible gasp of "Ahhhmmm" when she caught sight of Bali for the second time. "He is so cute!" she exclaimed, completely enamored by the little bundle of fluff before her. And she wasn't alone—everyone at the terminal felt their hearts swell with adoration upon seeing the small, tricolor Gales Cardigan Corgi puppy. A dark black back and light fawn fluffy fur accented his white chest and kind of golden face, while his left blue eye sparkled like the sky on a perfect summer day. Snow-white paws peeked out from under his body, making it impossible to resist his undeniable charm.

The process of selecting Bali as their newest family member had been relatively short but involved much careful thought. Now that he was in front of them, they knew they had made the right choice. This fluffy little Corgi was the perfect addition to their household and would bring endless joy to their lives, or so they thought.

To welcome and help him settle in, Dr. Tatiana purchased a gourmet meal and tasty treats for small-breed dog food online. She also ordered a cake with the new puppy's face for Bali's homecoming. It was a small family celebration, aware that Bali was arriving at a new residence and might still be confused and disoriented. Nevertheless, they should celebrate the occasion as they have embraced a new family member in their home.

— — —

Back to the present time, seven and a half months later, with our two amigos.

As our little scammers sprinted through the bustling bullet train station, Ben's heart raced with adrenaline as he whispered a hasty plan to Ginger to avoid being caught. They hastily agreed on a designated meeting point in New York City, their minds buzzing with the urgency of their mission. Seated inside the train, they nervously scanned the crowded coach class, carefully choosing seats far enough apart to blend in with the other passengers. Underneath one of their seats sat Bali, his small puppy carrier in front of Ginger's jacket and handbag. The energetic dog whined as he wanted to greet every person who walked by.

No matter Bali's impulses, Ginger had secured him tightly, determined not to let him run off and ruin their cover. As the train picked up speed and crossed into American territory, they thought they were in the clear. However, when they were finalizing the customs paperwork, suddenly and without warning, a fierce snowstorm descended upon them.

Some forecasts mentioned hail for that day, but nothing was said about snow. The snow was so thick and heavy that it felt like trying to run through a wall of white. Despite Amtrak's preparations for the journey ahead, they were unprepared for this intense storm that seemed determined to stop them in their tracks. With every step they needed to take to complete their immigration procedures, the snow piled higher and higher around them, threatening to bury them alive.

A gentle snowfall at the beginning became a storm and blanketed the town, quickly transforming into a raging blizzard. The meteorologists, indeed, had forecasted hail. They never foresaw this developing into an unexpected snowstorm, and its icy embrace encompassed everything in its path. The trees, with their branches burdened by the weight of heavy snow, bent and groaned as if begging for mercy. The bitter wind whipped around viciously, reducing visibility to mere inches.

Once everyone completed their business with customs, those trains' skilled and experienced pilots sprang into action—deactivating the autonomous system and taking control to navigate the treacherous conditions. They never received a warning about this weather situation. Apparently, this condition developed unpredictably. As they pushed forward, large snowflakes cascaded from the sky, twirling and swirling in a mesmerizing dance before finally settling on every surface. The landscape was transformed into a stunning winter wonderland, but this was no peaceful scene—the wind howled like a fierce beast, creating spiraling eddies of snow that seemed to have a life of their own.

Under feet of snow, drivers and their passengers in any kind of vehicle were frantically attempting to free themselves from the snow. At least getting out of their cars to find refuge. The flying cars couldn't pass through the heavy snow as it rapidly accumulated in their propellers. Soon enough, the Emergency Response Office issued a driving ban for the area. Amid the chaos, the big snowplow trucks, the electric company trucks, and the gas company trucks rushed to the streets to resolve the damages to their installations. The heavy trucks of the fire department and some jet skis equipped with medical things were used as improvised ambulances to help those in need.

Despite being bundled up in layers of clothing and huddled inside their homes, the cold still seeped through every structural fissure in every home. Shivers racked even the bravest of souls as they braced against gusts of wind, reaching speeds of 111 to 148 miles per hour (178.64 to 238.18 kilometers per hour). Amid all this fury of nature, one could have a glimmer of hope—the brave emergency response teams working tirelessly to provide aid and comfort to those affected by the storm in no time.

The snowfall continued to climb at an alarming rate—100 inches per hour (254 centimeters per hour)—and coupled with the powerful winds, towering drifts began to form, reaching heights of 39 to 49 feet (11.89 to 14.94 meters). This was a rare occurrence—not witnessed since the notorious 1977 storm that struck 73 years ago. This time, the snowstorm condensed what had taken days to strengthen into mere hours of utter chaos and destruction, underscoring the unprecedented scale of the event.

As the blizzard raged on, all emergency service centers sprang into action with an urgency never seen before. Authorities quickly halted vehicular traffic, allowing only rescue vehicle operators to brave the treacherous streets of Downtown Buffalo, New York. The snowplows worked tirelessly, their blades cutting through the thick layers of snow with a determination matched by none. In a matter of hours, the Buffalo Police in New York State, the Militias from all military branches, and the National Guard were all mobilized to assist in the ongoing crisis.

In the year 2051, the population of the city of Buffalo, NY, and its closed vicinities reached 1,980,000. This unexpected storm (that should have been hail) was causing significant damage to this region. Local news channels covered the incident from every angle to keep residents informed. Channel Two, 'WGRZ, 2 on your side,' deployed a fleet of twelve drones with anti-humidity lenses to capture images of the weather and those affected by the storm. Meanwhile, Channel Four, 'WIVB, 4 Warn Weather,' in addition to the drones and reporters, sent their electric helicopter equipped with dual rotors and hot air fans to monitor the storm activity and what could be expected in the coming hours.

Channel Seven, 'WKBW, 7 News Team,' was the first to conduct live interviews of drivers stranded in the snow and families trapped by the blizzard. Reporters from the National Public Radio-NPR were also present. They launched a small campaign to mobilize citizens into action. They stressed the importance of small contributions on radio as much as television. Their slogan was: "You don't need to make an extraordinary effort to help. Look for small opportunities to lend a hand to others."

The formal and informal media did an extraordinary job of informing the population and contacting the help needed to save lives. A lot of people were helping their neighbors, demonstrating the true spirit of Buffalo's motto, 'The City of Good Neighbors.' Buffalo Mayor Mr. Cleveland XII gave a live report through CNN, in the presence of NBC, CBS, and ABC from Williamsville, NY, as all access to City Hall Downtown was covered with piles of snow.

Major retail chains, including Walmart, Target, and Wegmans, also provided food and hot drinks to those affected by the devastating storm. Pepsi and Coca-Cola also made generous contributions, as did other important regional companies. The city of Buffalo in New York was embodying the message of its motto like never before.

The Buffalo General Medical Center and ECMC Health Campus were working at total capacity to help those affected. These two flagship health departments of the City of Buffalo and Erie County in New York treated everyone affected by the blizzard, with or without health insurance, subsidized by federal and state funds. This was because discussions about global health insurance in America were still ongoing, and it seemed like there was no hope that a universal healthcare system would ever be possible.

Furthermore, some heroic actions made headlines. First, there was the feat of the African American police officer Steve Johnson, who, without a second thought, dove under a massive pile of snow to rescue from their school bus the Buffalo Academy of Science Charter School students. Nearly suffering from hypothermia, he continued to rescue students two or three at a time until he managed to get all the twenty-five students, the driver, and an auxiliary for special ed students out of the pile of snow.

Second, the Ecuadorian American, the Principal of PS 095 Waterfront Elementary School, who decided to cook for a week out of her pocket to donate hot meals to the victims. Third was the story of the Burmese American Thura, who, along with his seven crewmembers from his restaurant in downtown Buffalo, shoveled snow from the driveways of more than a hundred homes in three days of work.

As the havoc continued downtown Buffalo, about seven and a half miles (12.07 kilometers) outside the city limits, the bullet train chugged along its tracks in the middle of the chaos unfolding around it. As it entered the village of Sloan, New York, it became hopelessly stuck in a mound of snow on a frozen snow base. The authorities immediately deployed a specialized rescue service to aid the stranded passengers, providing warm blankets and nourishing hot drinks to stave off the biting cold of the early night. The city encountered a winter that had been forgotten for quite some time.

Throughout the long and brutal night, emergency and rescue services worked tirelessly, braving the unforgiving conditions to clear roads, transport victims to shelters, and rescue those injured in the storm. As dawn broke on the next day, emergency and rescue services continued their operations without rest, bringing more and more people to clinics, hospitals, warm emergency centers, and refuge centers for essential care.

Finally, after a grueling wait that lasted well past noon, officials set a plan to transport passengers from the bullet train to motels in the northern part of the city. Strangely enough, the unrelenting snowfall merely spared this area, providing a small beacon of hope amid an otherwise dire situation.

Even two days after heavy cleaning, it was obvious that the Buffalo metropolitan area had been heavily affected by the brutal snowstorm. In the north of the city, early in the morning, Ginger strolled with Bali through a small and colorful village nestled in the north region outside the City of Buffalo. Feeling more adventurous than usual, the little dog forced Ginger to take an adventurous path at sunrise, excited about unfamiliar sights and experiences. As they made their way down the winding streets, his nose twitched with delight at all the unfamiliar scents that filled the air. However, it wasn't until he arrived at a charming park in the heart of Williamsville village that Ginger spotted something genuinely captivating for him.

A young woman with long red chestnut hair and a bright smile was taking her furry companion for a walk. She caught sight of Ginger and exclaimed, "What a cute little dog! What breed is he?" "Well, he is a Corgi… not sure if he is a Cardigan or Pembroke Welsh," Ginger responded. "It seems to be a Cardigan because of his tale and big ears," the young lady replied without hesitation. She turned back to have a good look at Ginger's eyes. Then she added: "You seem to be a good boy, so let me tell you this. Your kindness to dogs always comes back to you." These are words that Ginger never thought he would hear from a young, beautiful woman. Or it could be that he never thought about the young woman's intellectual capacity since he could not get over his fascination with her charms.

From the moment Ginger saw her, he was captivated by her warmth and apparent sensitivity. This prompted him to trot with Bali to greet her. Happily, Bali turned out to be a good bait for the young woman to take, and he got the chance to talk to her. The two bonded over their love for dogs and soon found themselves engrossed in lively conversation. As they chatted, both of them absentmindedly guided their dogs along on their leashes. The park had a fenced area where the doggies could be left loose and play freely and they decided to put them there to chat at ease. The difference was that the other dog, familiar with the area from their daily walks, knew precisely where to go while Bali was disoriented, but he wisely followed closely behind the other dog.

Then, Bali became distracted by a sudden burst of sound, maybe a distant dog bark or the alluring scent of something delicious in the air. In an instant, he darted off with excited abandon, swiftly disappearing into the dense foliage of nearby bushes. Right there where it was a hole in the metal mesh, from where he agilely went out in his curiosity to explore. His agile movements and sleek form were barely visible among the tangled branches and leaves as if he had become one with the wild surroundings until disappearing from the scene.

Ginger and the new girl clicked together effortlessly; their personalities blended seamlessly in an instant. At that moment, an atmosphere of camaraderie and gallantry filled the air, as if they were old friends meeting again after a long time apart. Laughter and smiles flowed freely between them, their spirits lifting higher with each passing moment. It was a bond that seemed like an unrealistic dream, a connection built on mutual understanding and aspirations. And as they walked arm in arm, it felt like romance was hovering around. Unfortunately, this loving encounter would very quickly bring Ginger kisses and tears. Due to his carelessness, Bali ran away, and he never thought he would end up loving a small canine companion as much in such a short time.

Panic surged through Ginger's veins as he scanned the area, his heart hammering against his chest. Where was Bali? He tore through the bushes, frantically calling out for his canine companion, but it was all in vain. His new friend helped him out as well, with no luck. Twenty-two agonizing minutes passed before it hit him—Bali was gone. With tears in his eyes, Ginger refused to give up, desperately searching for any sign of this new friend. He could only pray that Bali would find his way back to the motel, their safe-haven refuge, before it was too late for Bali to find his way back to him.

— — —

Meanwhile, now at the Wojcik's residence.

Engineer Barbara Smith took her usual exit off the bustling freeway after a long work night at the plant, where an emergency required her assistance. She turned onto a quiet backstreet leading to her quaint neighborhood a few miles from the village's park from where Bali had just escaped. She noticed the traffic light was out as she approached the intersection where a side street met a secondary road. She cautiously glanced in every direction to ensure no other cars were approaching the convergence. In her focused state, she barely registered the playful figure of Bali, a very naughty dog trotting across the street from east to west at the other end.

She was so absorbed in making sure she had a clear path that she didn't even notice Bali's presence as he reached the front yard of the corner house on the other side of the street. Her quick reflexes and feminine intuition kicked in as she glimpsed Bali's black back through her peripheral vision. She slammed on the brakes as she was almost on the other side of the intersection. Without her knowing it, this split-second decision saved Bali's life as he scurried silently toward a home conveniently located right next to Barbara's house.

Feeling relieved and slightly shaken, Barbara took a moment to catch her breath before continuing on her way. However, her curiosity got the best of her, and she pulled over to investigate what caught her eye. As she peered out of her car window, all she could see was a deserted street. Had it been a shadow or a stray animal? Assured that everything was alright, she continued driving and soon arrived at her own home.

Before parking in her garage, Barbara stepped out of her car and looked around for any signs of what had grabbed her attention earlier. Finding nothing, she shook it off and pressed the button on her remote control to open the garage door. The clicker was not working, so she knew she must open the door manually. As she drove into her cozy abode, Barbara couldn't avoid feeling relieved and liberated from the idea of having ended the life of an animal - not knowing that she indeed saved the life of Bali, such an adorable canine.

– – –

Concurrently, in Seoul, South Korea, a little later that day, but in 2042.

While filming the popular South Korean soap opera "Kisses and Tears," a sudden commotion arose as a small tri-color Corgi trotted onto the set. The actors were taken aback, their perfect lines and performances momentarily forgotten as they gazed at the adorable dog walking among them with a sacred air. Bali's excited barks and howls echoed throughout

190

the set, adding an unexpected soundtrack to the scene being filmed. The cast and crew were unsure of what to do with this unexpected visitor, but they continued to act out their lines, incorporating the little puppy's presence into the performance.

Bali stumbled into the scene, his head spinning and his senses overwhelmed. As he stepped into the filming scenario, he couldn't help but feel disoriented. The people around him seemed just as nervous, but their welcoming smiles and genuine gestures eased his apprehension. He was drawn to their warmth and immediately began to interact with them. The filming studio buzzed with energy and excitement. Bali couldn't contain his delight, and his contagious positive attitude spread to everyone he encountered in the lively atmosphere.

As the assistants to the director and producers frantically checked their notes, the director's anger boiled over, demanding to know whose visitor came with a doggy as 'A Tourist in "Kisses and Tears,"' that evening.

"Who had allowed their pet to interrupt the filming?" That was in his mind. However, he refrained from shouting "Cut!" for fear of disrupting the scene flow they were about to finish.

Amid the chaos, the production manager and his assistants couldn't avoid smiling at Bali's friendly demeanor. The assistant director saw an opportunity in this unforeseen circumstance and urged everyone to wait and see if they could use it to their advantage. After all, as he always said, "What if this accident turns out to be a stroke of luck? That is true live filmmaking."

This small and scruffy dog bounded into the scene with an infectious excitement that captivated the actors, producers, and writers. His fluffy tail wagged furiously as he weaved through the group, his tongue lolling out of his mouth in pure joy at being surrounded by so many people. Bali's soft fur brushed against the actresses' legs and the actors' pants with each playful leap and dash around the set. No one minded—how could they when they were all smiling at this adorable canine who had brought such life and energy to their day? As sunlight filtered onto the set through a small skylight in the roof, Bali's golden facial fur shone like a ray of sunshine, adding more brightness to the already vibrant scene.

Bali pranced around the set, his fluffy tricolor fur bouncing with each step. He seemed oblivious to the chaos he had caused, his wagging tail giving away his excitement. The tension in the air only fueled his enthusiasm as every sound and movement caught his keen senses. Bali's attention slowly and inevitably focused on the leading actress as the actors struggled to continue their scripts. His sudden appearance took her aback, but she couldn't suppress her laughter at the playful Corgi causing mayhem on set.

Bali's contagious energy quickly infected everyone present as he happily explored every nook and cranny of the set. Trying a closeup, a cameraman discovers his name, Bali, as he can read it from his name tag. He immediately announced it to the actors through the prompts installed in every corner and each side of the set. The initially thrown-off actors soon adapted and incorporated mentions of Bali into their lines, adding a layer of charm to the soap opera scene. Bali saw an opportunity to run toward the leading actress, planting a wet kiss on her cheek with his tongue lolling out in a goofy grin.

Despite the director's frantic gestures to stop him, Bali continued to spread joy wherever he went. The crew rushed to adjust lighting and camera angles, capturing Bali's impromptu performance for eternity. The usually dreadful Director couldn't avoid grinning as he watched Bali chase his tail in the background, stealing the spotlight from everyone else on the set.

In the end, everyone on set laughed, even the spectators who were present in that day's filming. And they all laughed so much and hard at Bali that the film studio erupted into one laugh. It was a contagious laughter that made even those who had finished laughing start again from the infection of others. When it seemed impossible to calm the collective laughter, they began crying with deep tears one by one, and the dry laughter turned into sobbing tears. Until they had no more tears left, they all cried their eyes out.

Yet, the tears didn't seem to accumulate on the studio floor; instead, they dissipated or evaporated at the touch of the ground. Maybe the heat was flowing from the underground of Seoul, South Korea, because it didn't matter that the air conditioning was working to its maximum capacity. It was as if a collective memory of everyone who loved a lost and later found pet materialized in the tears of all. It wasn't until Bali calmed down and sat back on his hind legs forty-two minutes later that they began shaking off the trance they had fallen into and returned to themselves in the present moment of the filming event.

As it happened to the camera crew, Bali's leap onto the set left the South Korean actors momentarily frozen in awe. But the actors and camera operators quickly sprang into action to capture every moment. As fate would have it, the director ended up so enchanted by Bali's presence that he decided to include him in the scenes. So, Bali unwittingly became a crucial part of that day's filming, stealing the hearts of the cast and the lucky viewers who witnessed his impromptu performance on the set.

The Epilogue

The first lights of dawn peeked over the horizon again, casting a warm golden glow over the quaint streets of East Amherst, New York, in 2051. Charming residencies lined up with the roads, their windows sparkling with the golden light of dawn as if they were the first to be touched by the sun's rays. A sense of calm filled the air, belying the bustling activity inside one particular residence, where a family of scientists and engineers worked tirelessly in their not-so-modest in-home laboratory.

They reside in the alluring East Amherst, a suburban hamlet in Erie County, 16 miles (25.75 km) northeast of downtown Buffalo, New York. On that warm winter morning, they were busier than usual. Right there at home, innovation and hard work collided in a beautiful symphony on that quiet sunrise. Besides, that was the same dawn when Eng. Barbara almost ran over Bali unintentionally. On that same aurora, her husband and son-in-law were hard at work in their laboratory, trying to give the final touch to an invention that could revolutionize the package delivery industry.

Their installation had expanded thanks to advancements in computing and technology, granting access to more advanced capabilities for those with exceptional intellectual capacity. There they were, engineering a sub-nanoparticle transferring or teleporting machinery, a marvel of human ingenuity that could also become a time travel machine—who knows? It was a labyrinth of wires and circuits, humming with pulsating energy that crackled with the promise of traversing through the folds of time itself. Large high-voltage cables arranged in circuits explicitly designed to powered this machine. Its sleek metal body seemed to shine with radiance as it held the secrets of the universe. Awaiting there to be discovered by these scientists with exceptional minds.

That early morning, the air was thick with the scent of metal and electricity, and the low hum of machinery filled the office laboratory room. Dr. Brian carefully maneuvered through the cluttered space, narrowly avoiding a collision with delicate instruments as he worked on connecting the components for their project. His father, Dr. Wojcik, and brother-in-law, the Mechanic Engineer Enilton, were deep in conversation - discussing valuable instructions provided by Enilton over their holographic cellphone.

They fully engrossed themselves in their latest endeavor - the sub-nanoparticle transferring machine that promised to revolutionize package delivery and possibly travel through teleporting. Every detail followed the precise schematic created by none other than Dr. David himself, who meticulously planned and executed them with the help of his son, Dr. Brian. Despite knowing the slim chances of successfully transferring or teleporting back in time, they remained determined not to rule out the possibility. Even if they couldn't achieve that feat, they were confident in their ability to create a future where transferring or time travel is possible for all.

Whiirrrrr! Suddenly, the screech of a hard brake was heard in the distance. The faint sound of this commotion outside the house caught Dr. Brian's attention, causing him to look up through the window in front of his workbench at the interconnected, multilevel basement. However, he couldn't glance at anything. He turned to his father, Dr. David, with a curious expression and asked, "What do you think happened out there, Dad?" Dr. Wojcik, the father, smiled warmly and replied, "Oh, it's probably only a minor mishap. Let's not worry about it and focus on finishing our project." Despite his lingering curiosity, Dr. Brian heeded his father's advice, and they returned to delicately piecing together the intricate components of their machinery.

The clinks and clanks of metal against metal filled the air as they worked together in comfortable silence after receiving wise instructions from the engineer Enilton. Thus, the only perceptible sounds were those of their tools and the occasional distant traffic of vehicles moving in the distance outside the house.

Father and son delved deep into the intricate theory of sub-nanoparticle transfer and the possibility of time travel, their heated discussions echoing off the walls as they tried to unravel the possibility of returning to the present after traveling to the future given that moving to the past have been proven almost impossible. As Brian's mind raced with plans for his journey through time, the weight of potential consequences kept him up at night, tossing and turning in a restless state of fear and excitement. The idea of altering the fabric of time consumed his every thought, leaving him haunted by doubts and questions that refused to let him rest.

They clearly understood the quantum mechanics of transferring objects broken down into particles smaller than sub-atoms. That was not such a problem, nor was the creation of magnetic fields to speed up the rotatory revolutions of the machine without the friction that could overheat the system. All that physical theory was now logical. "How would this alter the course of history itself because of an intervention in the development of the daily events of life?" Dr. Brian asked his dad seriously that morning: "We are uncertain if the future is in a present status in another dimension or if it does not exist," David responded.

They were debating about the possibilities of not only transferring to specific destinations but also opening the boundaries to transfer or teleport at different times, as in time travel. "So, where would the transfer arrive? It was Brian's rebuttal. They both know that there is not a simple answer. "It could remain hanging in the cosmos, or it could vanish before the transformation of the nanoparticles could re-materialize," David concluded. "Enough of discussion!" David emphatically abrupted the conversation. "Let's return to the activity at hand," he concluded.

So, because of a garage door clicker malfunction, Eng. Barbara pushed up her individual garage door to open it. Immediately, a flash of a black blemish caught her eye. She peered into the dimly lit space, hoping to catch another glimpse of the mysterious creature. Turning on the overhead light, she cautiously entered, her heart racing excitedly. As she reached the spot where she had seen the blurred black blemish, it was nowhere to be found. Confusion crept over her; "Could it have been a trick of the light?" she thought. With determination, she searched the front yard and then expanded her search to the neighboring yards, trudging through wet grass and mud in her favorite shoes.

Barbara's shoes were her trusted companions, now their soles covered in mud and the fabric stained from her impromptu pursuit of the elusive creature. They were also a tangible representation of her fierce determination and daring spirit, having endured countless trips over the years of camping with her group of Girl Scouts. Every scratch and mark told a story of Barbara's unwavering passion for discovery and her unwillingness to back down from any challenge.

Rebounding to Dr. David's Office—also known as his laboratory—he and his son Dr. Brian, both esteemed doctors in Quantum Mechanics, were hard at work on their latest invention: the "Electromagnetic Teleportation Machine of Basic Chemical Sub-Nanoparticles," or "ETRAMOBCHESNA" for short. They preferred that name instead of the simplistic 'teleporting machine' as it truly detailed the intricacies of the intended purposes. The room hummed with buzzing computers and intricate machinery as they meticulously tinkered and tested their creation. This was their passion—pushing the boundaries of science and unlocking new possibilities to reach new scientific discoveries.

Dr. Brian's girlfriend, computer engineer Jennifer Williams, looked after and maintained the computers in the lab. She also services all the computer software packages. Jennifer was also passionate about South Korean soap operas. She never missed a single opportunity to delight in watching them on television or on her cellphone and immersing herself in their love intrigues. She loves romances with all the disappointments, betrayals, kisses, tears, and sentimental struggles.

Regardless of all his close collaborators, Dr. David never expected or even imagined his former colleague from the university, Dr. Motuo Locus, and his accomplice in espionage efforts, Mrs. Marsha Ponzi, or better said 'Lila,' to monitor his laboratory's events secretly. As it turned out, Marsha had planted a hidden camera on a day when nobody was paying much attention. Obviously, the sound and small writing on a computer screen were always impossible to decipher. Though David and Motuo had worked together on their doctoral and post-doctoral thesis on transferring sub-nanoparticles at the University of Buffalo, Dr. David and Dr. Motuo became unrevealed rivals after completing their post-doctoral studies. However, in public and whenever one mentioned the other, they maintained the facade of a close friendship to uphold professional appearances.

Dr. Motuo had tried to take all the credit for the research in common with Dr. David. Still, the second was the one who held the key to solving the puzzle of reunification or regrouping the molecular structure of the sub-nanoparticles before and after being transferred. That was why Motuo wanted to take possession of his notes, to conquer this impossible dream and claim total success. Somehow, only teamwork with highly trained professionals allowed David to solve such a complicated phenomenon. Thus, after so many hours of insomnia and long hours of work without rest, he was about to reach the pinnacle of success without knowing it. Despite being close to materializing his dreams, he kept the candor from when he became interested in quantum mechanics to help solve pressing problems that technological advances brought to human civilization.

Unaware of other ongoing conflicts discussed in the lab about the relationship between Wojcik and Locus and all the activity enclosed in David's laboratory, Bali did his best to stay composed when he sneaked into his house and walked to his lab. Bali's heart pounded relentlessly in his chest as he cautiously entered the house through the garage. He knew this was unknown territory, and he had to remain silent and observant rather than his usual festive and amicable self. With swift and precise movements, he made his way through the mezzanine and onto the first floor, a fearless determination driving him forward to uncover the mystery of these strangers. As he approached the open doorway, his senses were on high alert, scanning for any signs of danger.

The distant echoes of voices only added to the tension, sending shivers down Bali's spine as he carefully made his way toward Dr. Wojcik's office. Keeping a safe distance, he observed the doctor and his assistant working feverishly, their movements quick and urgent. Every fiber of Bali's being was on edge, ready for whatever may come next. After months of intense training, he had finally mastered control over his instincts and was able to maintain a calm exterior appearance, no matter the tense situation. Even so, deep down, his genuine inner desire was to play freely with everyone who approached him.

Bali's heart thudded against his ribcage, a mix of exhilaration and fear coursing through his veins as he peered at them from the depths of the shadows. His entire body trembled with anticipation as he watched their nimble hands deftly manipulate strange objects and tinker with mysterious machines scattered around the room. The air was thick with tension as snippets of their urgent conversation reached his ears, making him feel like an outsider in this clandestine world.

Suddenly, Dr. Brian froze in mid-sentence and scanned the room, his piercing gaze settling on the shadows where Bali hid. For a moment, Bali feared he would be discovered; straight away, the sound of the garage door slamming shut reverberated through the space, distracting Dr. Brian. "Is that you, Mom?" he called out, relief evident in his voice. "Yes, it's me!" Bali heard the tone of her reply with a sense of calm, yet deep down, he couldn't shake off the unease that lingered as he remained hidden in the shadows.

Engineer Barbara entered the house and immediately closed the door that give access to the garage. Her son Brian perked up at the sound and eagerly awaited his mother's arrival inside the house and, later on, to the lab. Barbara climbed the stairs to the first floor, passed the kitchen, and once near the lab, she made her presence known to her husband and stepson, who were already waiting for her.

"Ohhh!" she exclaimed at something that caught her attention. As she glanced back at the entrance door from the garage to the kitchen, this was wide open. This detail struck her as odd since she and her husband, David, had discussed their preference for keeping it closed at all times. David adamantly believed that leaving it open would waste precious heat or air conditioning.

Bali, who usually loved welcoming visitors with a wag of his tail, cowered and slinked away from the tense atmosphere in the house today. Not tense by any irrational discussion, just by the uninterrupted activity of the scientists. David and Brian's ongoing conversation seemed to have put him on edge as he watched them from the sidelines talking about the 'ETRAMOBCHESNA' project they were working on together. As they huddled around the computer screens, finalizing details and plans for their invention, Bali crept towards the mysterious machine in the room's east corner.

At the time when David and Brian were about to begin a crucial test, Bali slipped inside a dark capsule unnoticed when someone knocked at the door of the Wojcik family. "Who could be at 8:20 in the morning," Dr. Davis shouted. So, sensing an opportunity for perhaps some relief from the tension in the air, Bali took the risk and got into the darkest corner of the machine that still was off. There was too much tension because the scientists were trying to push to the limit his efforts into putting the finishing touches on the machine that they thought would transfer sub-nanoparticles to different coordinates and maybe into the future; but how could Bali comprehend that?

— — —

Let's go back in time a little to illustrate Bali's behavior better. When he was three months old, Bali was a ball of energy, constantly chewing on anything he could get his teeth on. His favorite targets were law textbooks and, more

204

excitingly, medical books with colorful photos. He didn't discriminate against other objects either. Bali would also take long naps after bursts of energy, leaving his owners wondering what was happening in his little puppy brain. Bali's curiosity knew no bounds; he sniffed every kitchen corner and eagerly destroyed any unattended food packaging. His adventurous spirit even led him to sit on keyboards and accidentally delete or change essential legal notes or documents. So, Bali needed to be trained to control his impulses and be quiet for most of the day.

Since Bali underwent training with the best behavioral dog trainers available, he could control himself at will – whether he wanted to was another thing. His owners, Dr. Manuel and Dr. Tatiana, were unaware of this, and given that they were unsatisfied with his behavior, they persisted in training Bali until they could observe an improvement. So, Bali was still in training at seven and a half months old. Little did the Hashbuns know the training was already settled down on Bali's head—only if they could see it at Dr. Wojcik's residence that day.

– – –

Back to Dr. Wojcik's office lab.

With the rising sun's crisp on that Wednesday morning of January 25th, 2051, National Irish Coffee Day, one of Dr. David's former students humbly sought his professional advice. The student, filled with admiration for the professor's expertise, sought his guidance to analyze his study's data for the conclusions of his doctoral dissertation. As he knocked on the door, the sound echoed through the quiet walls of the living room through the kitchen. Unbeknownst to anyone, Bali used this distraction to hide in the machine, silently observing and carefully listening to the many events unfolding in the office laboratory in that residence.

"I apologize, Andres. Today is not a convenient day for this," replied David to the student's request for help. He left behind his notes, hoping Dr. David would find time to review them and provide valuable insights for completing his project in the coming days. Dr. David returned to his office lab and instructed Dr. Brian to initiate the sequence. "Did you check the machine," he asked her son. "Yes indeed, a few minutes ago," he replied. "Well, get ready," David added and accidentally touched a bottom when reaching for the object they were about to experiment with.

PuuuuuuuumN! A sudden, jarring, and loud sound echoed across the room. It sounded like a truck tire blowing out on the highway. The two doctors and the engineer gathered around the transferring or teleporting "ETRAMOBCHESNA" machine. Their faces were etched with concern as they reviewed its computational records. David furrowed his brow as he tried to explain the highly unusual activity the machine's computational records were showing.

Barbara and her stepson Brian exchanged bewildered glances, their minds reeling as they tried to make sense of what they had witnessed. Soon after, Barbara's voice cut through the tension as she turned to David and asked, "What did you transfer?" His response was uncertain as he replied, "Nothing yet."

Wait, hold both on to your thoughts for a second, Dr. Brian told his parents: "Well, it seems like whatever was teleported by the machine included the 'I-245678-M' microfiche."

"Do you say that the smart and self-generative of artificial intelligence microchip has disappeared?" Dr. David asked.

"How did you come up with the idea that it got transferred or teleported?" Eng. Barbara interjected.

"Well, it was inside this folder that I had in my hands the last time I entered the capsule. I'm well aware of that. So, it fell out of the folder and onto the floor inside the machine, as I don't see it on the floor or elsewhere; no doubt about it." Dr. Brian said.

Dr. Brian Wojcik bowed his head and hit his right hand against his right leg. Then he turned his head to the sides in despair and disapproval of the outcome. But suddenly, as if he had had an epiphany, he raised his head upwards and exclaimed in a hallelujah tone: "Luckily, Jennifer cloned it last week, and we have a copy in the safe."

"Wow, that's some luck," his stepmother Barbara concluded.

Brian solemnly looked his parents in the eyes and made the following comment: "Remember Heidegger: 'Who thinks great thoughts often makes great mistakes.'"

Immediately, David interjected: "I only hope we can fix any errors competently. So, as not to disturb the discourse of time."

Still, Dr. David and his family were unaware that Bali had been teleported to the closest dimension to them at that time. The dimension matched the soap opera playing on the living room's television. The Eng. Jennifer Williams, Dr. Brian's girlfriend, was completely absorbed in watching it. She got home from the gym, took a quick shower, and didn't even notice what was happening around her. This was a rerun of the award-winning South Korean soap opera "KISSES AND TEARS.

My Buddy Bali:
A fantasy book about the dog stories of a seven-month-old
Corgi puppy, full of surprises —Dr. T. Zalla.

Trivia About Corgis' Tails
by Onairan Seyer**

**W**hy do some Corgis have long tails while others have short ones or none?

The answer to this question boils down to their genetics, aesthetics, and traditions. Some breeders dock Corgi tails in the first week of birth, meaning they amputate them. In the past, people performed tail docking on Corgis to make herding easier and prevent potential injuries from getting caught in fences or branches. However, despite this practice, some Corgis are still born with long tails, while others may have short tails.

The main reason is that there are two distinct types of Corgis - those with fluffy, low-set tails and those with short, stubby ones held high. The differences between these two go beyond the tail length. The long-tailed Corgis are slightly taller and have longer, slender bodies than their shorter-tailed counterparts. In addition, those with short tails have a less prominent rib cage, giving them a rounder appearance.

The two main breeds of Corgis are the **Pembroke Welsh Corgi** and the **Cardigan Welsh Corgi**. The differences in tail characteristics between these two breeds will explain why some Corgis have tails and others do not.

- - -

Pembroke Welsh Corgi

Tail Docking: Pembroke Welsh Corgis had their tails docked (surgically shortened) a few days after birth. Historically, people practiced tail docking on Pembroke Welsh Corgis for various reasons, including adhering to breed standards, preventing injuries in working dogs, or for aesthetic reasons.

Natural Bobtail: Some Pembroke Corgis are born with a natural short tail or "bobtail" because of a genetic mutation. In these cases, the dog's tail is shorter than usual.

Undocked: In recent years, due to changing attitudes toward animal welfare and legal restrictions in some countries, more people are choosing to leave Pembroke Corgis with their natural, full-length tails.

- - -

Cardigan Welsh Corgi

Natural Tails: Unlike Pembroke, Cardigan Welsh Corgi dogs naturally have long, bushy tails. These dogs usually keep their full tails since people do not traditionally practice tail docking on them.

In summary, whether a Corgi has a short or average-sized tail depends on the breed (Pembroke or Cardigan), other genetic factors, and whether the dog underwent the tail docking traditional practice.

So, the answer to why some Corgis have long tails while others have short ones or none lies in genetics and varies depending on breed standards in different countries. For example, in the United Kingdom, the professional standard does not allow the breeding of long-tailed Corgis, while in the United States, the breeder can breed both short-tailed and long-tailed Corgis as they wish.

—

(**) Onairam Seyer is the former editor-in-chief of the out-of-circulating e-magazine "Pablar.Com," a monthly bilingual electronic magazine about cultural topics related to Latinos in the United States.

Afterword by
Enilda Mougenot Pires-PhD*

The entanglement of the fictional sequence of events in Leu Seyer's book My Buddy Bali tells the story of a puppy who yearns for freedom, a condition not too distant from his hunger for adventures and new emotions. In search of happiness, Bali seeks a way to escape the monotonous conditions of life. The main character's emotional journey, as he finds the reality from which he always tries to escape, is vibrant and is a poignant exploration of a human's condition. In this way, realism forages for the fantastic in which elements of reality mix with those of fantasy and dreams.

Leu Seyer uses a realistic style, objective language, detailed descriptions, and a small narrative space to criticize some irrational customs and values of everyday life. In this way, realism slips into the marvelous, in which the elements of reality mix with illusions, and everyone's dreams can alter the outcome of any event. For example, when we find two petty thieves in a seemingly hopeless predicament, fortune smiles upon them as the efforts of others converge, creating an almost miraculous shift in their circumstances and empowering them to continue pursuing their objectives.

Chapter Four: "They finally arrived at the dumpsters and hovered there for about an hour or a little more. When the thugs were going to leave the dumpsters, a sudden rush of people poured out of the restaurant's banquet; some doubled over and wretched into the parking lot [given the stomach pain]. It was like a scene from a comedy movie, with mass food poisoning striking all at once."

Also, with his expertly crafted hyperbole, he creates, with simple words, a stunning distortion of reality that radically distracts us from the detailed, grounded account of his descriptive narrative. His exaggerated account of events interweaves with what he had painted in vivid descriptions, adding layers of intensity to his already vibrant imagination. Through skillful manipulation of figurative language, he took his audience on a journey of heightened understanding of the fascinating possibilities from the basin of magical realism.

Chapter One provides a good example: "This [red] ball rolled down the highway, bouncing into every object it encountered. It bounced down the roads, passing over uneven grounds and street intersections, until the last spin reached the front of the corner side deck in the house of the little Corgi puppy's owners."

In his narrative of interrelated events, the author's imagination relies on a dreamed notion, transforming it into a cruel reality, as in Chapter Eight, when Barbara asks David, "What did you transfer?" His response was uncertain as he replied, "Nothing yet."

Dr. David was unaware that Bali had been transported to his closest dimension then. The dimension matched "the soap opera playing on the living room television [...] named Kisses and Tears." A transfer/departure that may lead to a permanent separation from the current world.

Magic Sphere as a portal to other worlds.

Source: [Premium Photo | Raster illustration of magic sphere in the botanical garden Portal in the clearing in the forest Magic realism science fiction portal to other world parallel worlds 3D artwork (freepik.com)](#)

Leu also combines tragedy with the elements of dramedy in the confluence with the South Korean Soap Opera "Kisses and Tears." He offers a connective glimpse of themes of love, friendship, family, and societal issues, blurring the fine lines between reality and imagination. As a whole, he generates a harmonious new narrative of a fantastic everyday life. Leu Seyer's writing is reminiscent of the experiments of the artistic avant-garde, as it is a style imbued with the desire to change reality.

For example, in Chapter Three: "When the vase fell, his grandmother's voice could be heard telling him: "Take care of your mother, my dear child." He wants to confront her, but after losing Bali and destroying the family's heritage, he wants to shift an unwanted reality that cannot be changed, and he ends up in only forbearance.

The author's gaze, as close to reality as possible, opposes romantic idealization by presenting Bali as a portrait of the impersonal mode, far from the narrator's figurative sense of our individual awareness and the perception of otherness. This technique allows the reader to engage with the character on a more realistic level.

This emerging evolution of representing reality transcends traditional factual depictions and incorporates elements of Magical Realism, primarily found in Spanish-speaking cultures. This advancement in storytelling combines reality with the fantastical possibilities of the surreal while maintaining a delicate balance between the two realms.

He pushes the limits of what is considered possible, sometimes even venturing into exaggerated descriptions. As a writer born in the Dominican Republic, Leu Seyer may one day become one of its esteemed exponents in the future.

Leu Seyer's writing is a breath of fresh air in the avant-garde literary movement, boldly pushing the boundaries and quietly challenging traditional norms. His unique style defies categorization and invites readers to question their perception of corporeality.

As one delves into his body of work, it becomes apparent that his approach is more dynamic than romanticized, inviting readers on a journey to the future within the magical realm. Diving into his innovative writing skills is a valuable and enriching experience, offering new insights and perspectives worth exploring.

—

(*) Enilda Mougenot Pires was born in Aquidauana, Brazil, and got a PhD in Literature from the University of Poitiers of Paris, France. She is a respected member of the 'Academia Mato-Grossense do Sul' of Literature and holds the esteemed position of Chair member. Besides her successful academic career, the Ministry of Education and Culture has acknowledged and recognized her writing abilities. Even after retirement, she continues influencing young minds through teaching, writing, and composition in Campo Grande, Brazil.

Acknowledgment

While the popular expression that "One cannot choose one's family" is true, it is not a less accurate fact that we can decide how much we will love them. After everything a family member has been through, living together and sharing daily insights, one cannot help but choose to love them. Not loving them will mean abandoning our home and never returning. Notwithstanding, if we keep a link to them, it is for what they mean to our lives.

As family members, we have the unwavering support of those closest to us, strengthening us. We are deeply grateful for this support, even when it sometimes leads to some dysfunction. No one has planned this, nor does one hope it will be any other way.

The best thing about family is that each member has witnessed daily hardships and joys in the most embarrassing and vulnerable moments. Still, in those terrible situations, one creates utter bonds. These reciprocal loves transform us into people with more strength and spirit. The members of our nucleus family are the ones truly responsible for our best feats. And when I say the members of our nucleus family, I also mean our loving pets.

They are not just animals, simply integral parts of our family, contributing significantly to our happiness and well-being and making our lives genuinely joyful. My prematurely deceased Corgi Billy, in particular, filled my family's lives with his love and companionship, bringing a sense of joy and well-being one cannot measure.

In this sense, Billy was that canine son who always waited for me, full of joy to play, no matter the day's misfortunes. I remember one particular day when he brought his collar to me, wagging his tail as if to say, "Let's forget our worries and go for a walk," if he could have spoken. He always made me and those close to him laugh, and he kept us in physical shape with the long walks he demanded and loved. Billy knew when to play with each family member and when to stay still in his corner to avoid being scolded.

He never turned down an invitation to walk or to spend time in the yard with us while we read our messages on our cell phones, played games, or watched TV on it. Billy showed us that his love for his family transcended the walls of our house. His unconditional love was visible in every family photograph and every event he accompanied us to attend - and he loved immensely the long walks on Halloween. Every morning during breakfast, when he sat down to eat with us in the kitchen, and every night when he slept in our bed, this will never fade from our memories.

We are deeply grateful and will always love you, Billy-Bali. Your love and companionship have enriched our lives in ways we cannot fully express. We thank you infinitely for being part of our family and for the love you gave us, too.

My Buddy Bali

It is such a fantastic voyage. The captivating and despicable characters keep you hooked until the last word—O. Wang.

www.ingramcontent.com/pod-product-compliance
Lightning Source LLC
Chambersburg PA
CBHW061734120626
46550CB00005B/1797